£3

EDINBURGH
The Old Town

EDINBURGH

The Old Town

Hamish Coghill

John Donald · Edinburgh

ACKNOWLEDGEMENTS

Every working day my steps take me into the Old Town of Edinburgh. There is barely a corner which has not a tale to tell, and in gathering together many of those stories, and looking at the present and future, I have been greatly helped and encouraged by several people.

My wife Mary has been an invaluable support, and John Tuckwell of John Donald Publishers, whose idea this book was, has provided the necessary enthusiasm to see it completed. To Brian Johnston for his maps, to Scotsman Publications Ltd who provided many of the photographs and to many friends who have expressed an ongoing interest in the project, my thanks.

ISBN 0 85976 289 0

Typesetting: Bookworm Typesetting Ltd., Edinburgh
Printed and bound in Great Britain by Bell & Bain Ltd.,
Glasgow

CONTENTS

Map 1. Location of Old Town within Edinburgh

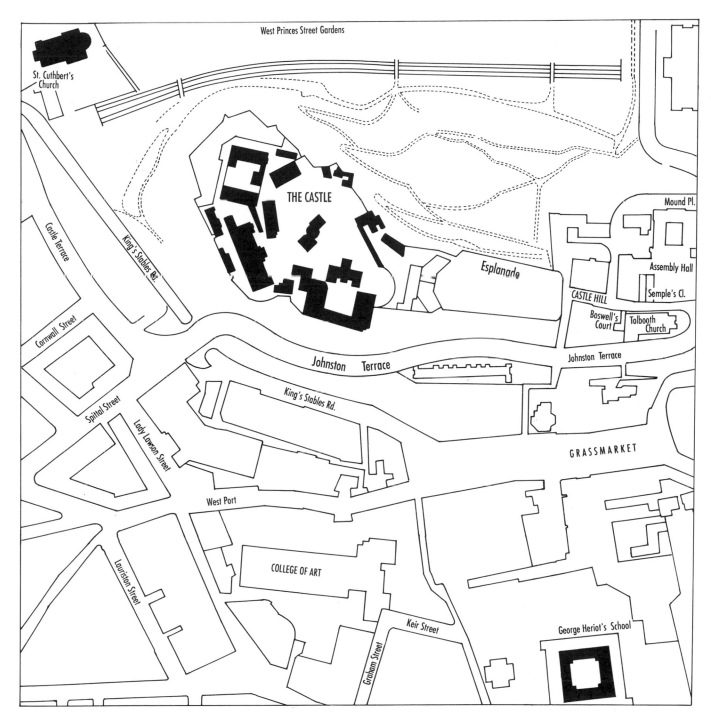

Map 2. Castle, Grassmarket and West Port

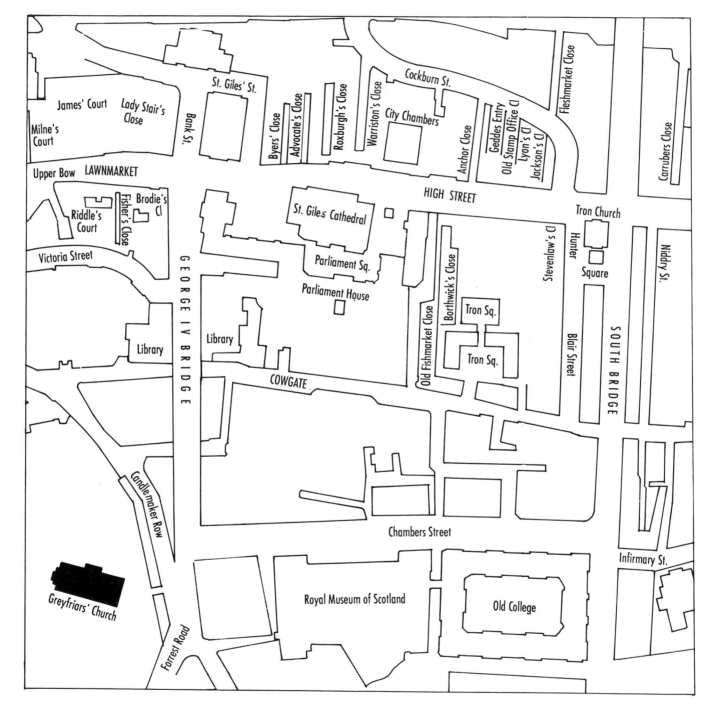

Map 3. Lawnmarket to South Bridge

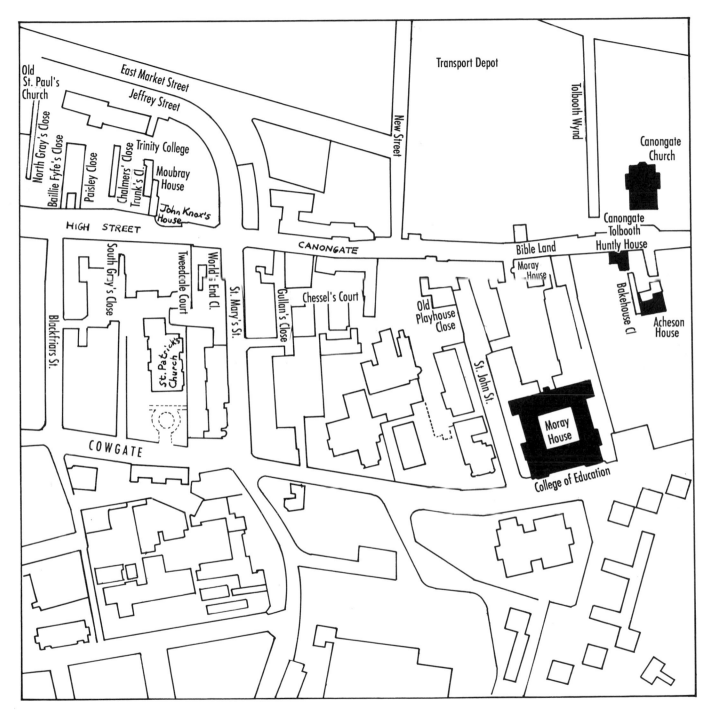

Map 4. High Street to Canongate

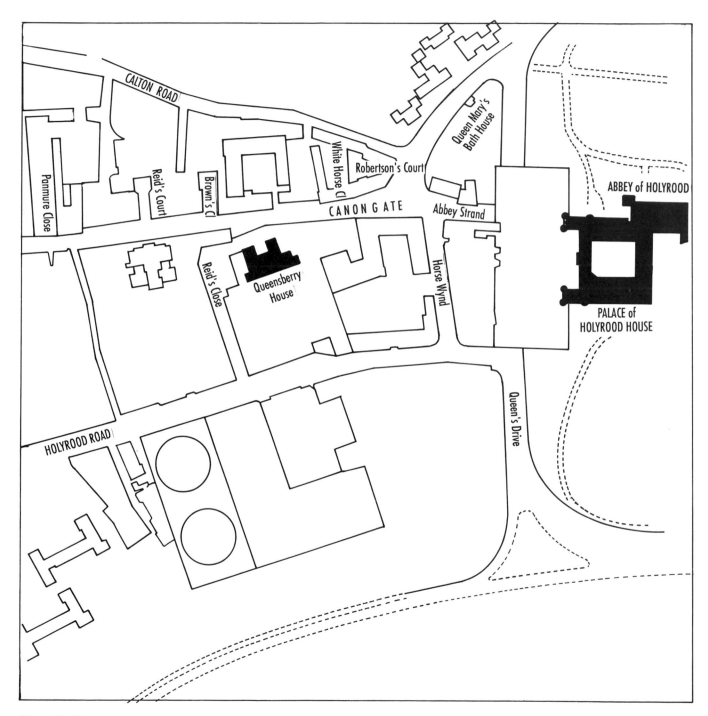

Map 5. Canongate to Holyrood Palace

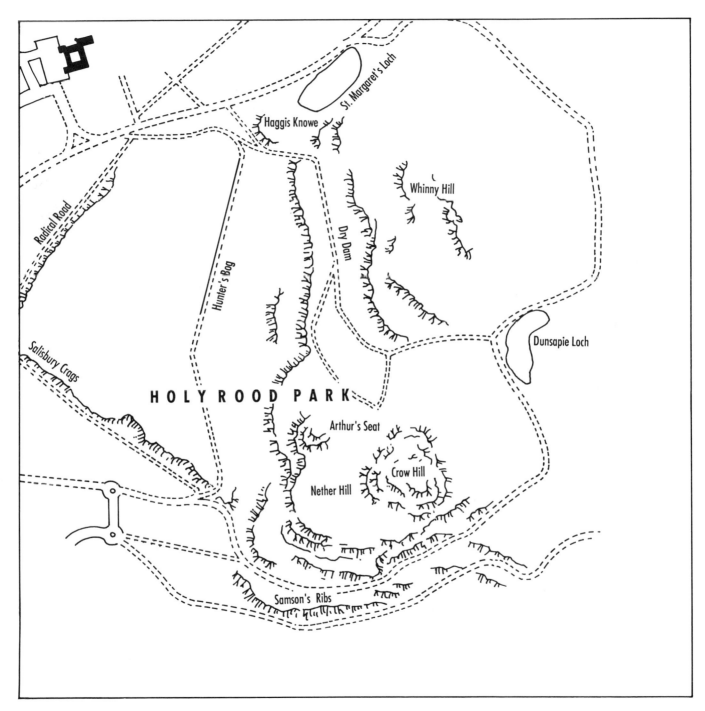

Map 6. Holyrood Park (Palace top left)

INTRODUCTION

*N*O ONE can say exactly when the first settlers arrived to find shelter on the huge extinct volcano rock which dominates the skyline of Edinburgh. No one can pinpoint when the first cluster of rude huts appeared round the protective crag on which the castle came to be formed, first a fortress, then a royal palace, and now a world-renowned attraction whose picture is synonymous with the city itself.

Tread the cobbles of the Royal Mile, the spine of the ancient city round which for centuries all its enterprises and inhabitants clung, and you touch on history at every step. Virtually every building has a tale to tell, or stands on a site where a piece of the city's fragmented story can be tracked. It is from this backbone that all other limbs stretch, down into the hinterland of the Cowgate and Grassmarket to the south through the steep chasms of closes and vennels, and the northwards arteries move into another, more sophisticated, separate Edinburgh – the New Town. This Royal Mile then stretches from the castle to the Royal residence of the Palace of Holyroodhouse at the foot of the slope, and measures as one mile and 106 yards from the inside of the drawbridge at the castle to the entrance door of Holyroodhouse.

It is still a living centre with new life flooding back as old tenements are renovated, and remember we had skyscrapers where rich and poor lived side by side on the same stair long before New York discovered high-rise building. The street changes name as it descends from Castlehill to Canongate, through the Lawnmarket and High Street, but the scene throughout is one of bustle and interest. It's a place where equally a few yards off the main thoroughfare you can find peace from the traffic noise or pedestrian crush, where a restful suntrap or a little garden makes a rewarding discovery. But the Royal Mile is only part of the Old Town, which was bounded to the north by a deep valley once filled by a stinking stretch of swamp and water – a valley now pierced by railway track and the Waverley Station, and disguised by ornamental gardens. To the south, and particularly in the area at the foot of the High Street closes, were packed the hardy citizens, and the ground rose yet again into the land now covered by the main buildings of the University before the city wall cut the town off from the country areas outside, maybe a mere half mile or so from the town's Mercat Cross.

Thus was Edinburgh clustered round the natural drawing place for its inhabitants, the ridge between castle and palace. And until 1767 when the need for an extension plan led to the creation of a second Edinburgh, and the city's subsequent expansions

Auld Reekie. The smoke and cloud hanging over Scotland's Capital gave the town its traditional name, but smoke control improvements have removed most of the reek, or smoke. Folk in Fife used to say they knew when it was dinner time in Edinburgh when they saw the smoke from thousands of fires pour from the chimneys.

in what we two centuries and more later still call the New Town, so it pretty well stayed. Between the natural barrier of the Nor' Loch and the several city walls the rumbustious, often dangerous and dramatically stimulating life of the Old Town was carried on.

To sample something of its past and present, you have to do a bit of exploring on your own. Look up and down from street level. There are carvings and stones, steeple and tower, old glass and handsome woodwork; signs now fading at close mouths; there is the parade of people, the lawyers heading for the courts, the Edinburgh matrons showing off their town to visitors, the nestling places of those down on

The crown spire of St Giles, the High Kirk of Edinburgh, and the steeple of the old Highland-Tolbooth Church dominate the upper stretch of the Old Town. In the foreground is the North Bridge, first built in 1763 to provide access to the land where the model New Town to the north would be built.

their luck; there is the subtle change that comes over the Old Town of an evening; and there is the inevitable spectator who sees all life passing by from the comfort of an open window.

Plunge down a steep close, or step into the calm of one of the open courts. Discover for yourself the mixture that makes Old Edinburgh.

For visitor and citizen alike the grandeur of the castle surpasses all as it stands proud in the heart of the city. From its ramparts is fired the one o'clock gun, Monday to Saturday, shaking the unwary and giving the town a very precise time signal. You can tell the natives by the way they check their watches.

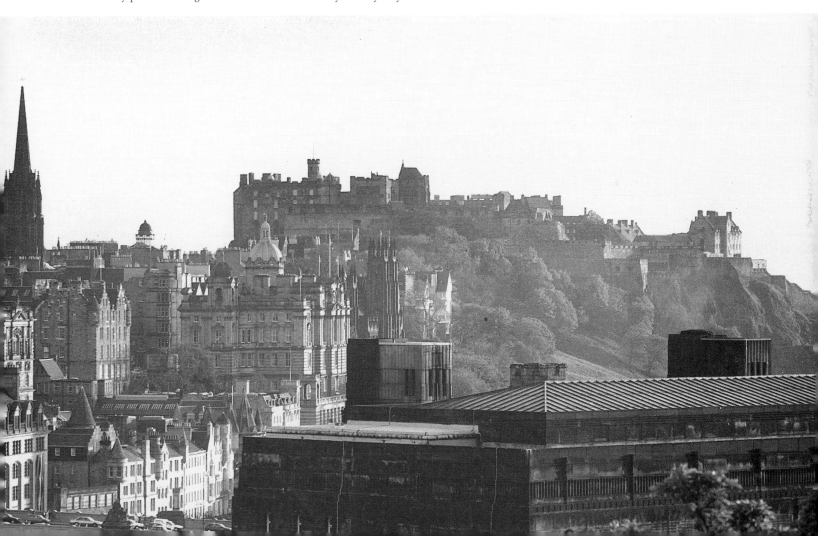

CHAPTER *1* # THE CASTLE

*T*HE CASTLE hangs over the whole of Edinburgh like some Disney cartoon –
but our castle is real. You have only to see and hear visitors catching their first
glimpse of it to know the impression it can make, although it must be said it can
be difficult to convince some tourists it does exist on a summer's day when our

The General Officer Commanding the Army in Scotland, holding the rank of Lieutenant-General, also
acts as Governor of Edinburgh Castle. The office was revived in 1936, and with due ceremonial he is
invested with the castle keys as an indication of his willingness to guard the fortress for the Queen.

celebrated haar (thick sea fog) has not yet been burned off by the sun. But the castle is one of those buildings which looks good in any weather and, of course, when it is floodlit it takes on another unequalled magical quality.

The citizens take it very much for granted, and since admission charges were introduced some years ago regular family outings to view the city from its battlements or to see the one o'clock gun fired are rare. So the voices that rend the air are likely to be those of tourists, lured to Britain's second most popular tourist attraction (the Tower of London is still No 1). But local folk do turn out in their thousands to support the renowned Military Tattoo at Festival time. Then the castle Esplanade is transformed into a majestic arena and a unique spectacle is presented against a backdrop of rampart and tower, lit and unlit as the performance dictates. The haunting skirl of the kilted pipers as they cascade over the moatbridge past the statues of Scotland's two heroes, William Wallace and Robert the Bruce, is deeply moving to a Scot and makes an indelible memory for the visitor.

A £6 million programme of improvements is now under way at the castle to make it more accessible and informative for visitors. In 1989 a start was made to driving a tunnel through the rock itself so that in due course pedestrians and vehicles will be segregated.

That rock can first be traced in a Welsh poem of the sixth century, the Gododdin of Aneurin, and a Pictish symbol stone of this period has been found by archaeologists. The name used by Aneurin was Dineidin, which translated into Gaelic becomes Dun-Eideann or Dunedene which in English is 'The Maidens' Castle', but whatever its origins it is evident that the town's name came from the fortification.

Stand on the battlements, or even the Esplanade, and look in every direction and you get an idea of just how important a fortress on such a rock was. There were many hill-forts in the Lothians, but Edinburgh alone dominated the point where the Roman route from the south reached the Firth of Forth.

'Here is, then, the appropriate point of concentration for trade and political influence, however irregular the one or shadowy the other, in an age when these things were inevitably centred in a chieftain's stronghold,' says one commentary. Because of such a strategic position the early Edinburgh survived when other Dark Age sites went out of existence.

Thus the rock called to its lea and security the settlers of Lothian. The first buildings would have nestled on the eastern slopes, the 'tail' of the crag and tail geological formation which is the rock and Royal Mile.

Within the castle walls stands St Margaret's Chapel, generally regarded as the oldest building in the city. It was probably constructed as a memorial to the deeply religious queen, who was already near her death when her husband Malcolm set

Outside Scotland's Shrine, the National War Memorial, the crowds and military pay tribute to the war dead. The Memorial was opened in 1927 and is the latest of the buildings in Crown Square in the heart of the Castle, standing on the site of a medieval church.

forth on his fifth and last invasion of England, by one of her younger sons David, who became King in 1124. Margaret was recognised as a saint in 1251, and at one time a number of buildings on the rock bore her name. The chapel went out of religious use after the Cromwellian siege; it was rediscovered in 1845 and restored a few years later. It is still used for marriage ceremonies by soldiers stationed in *The Castle* the castle, christenings and on other occasions, and it is a particular attraction for many visitors.

In the spring of 1296 Edward I of England successfully attacked Edinburgh Castle, using hurling machines to shower the garrison with a non-stop cascade of stones. They lasted only three days and nights under the onslaught. From Edinburgh, Edward, who earned the accolade (outside Scotland) of 'The Hammer

The magic moment of the Military Tattoo as the pipes and drums cascade over the castle bridge and onto the Esplanade. Scotland's heroes, King Robert the Bruce and Sir William Wallace, stand on either side of the gateway beneath the floodlit battlements.

of the Scots', took the Stone of Destiny – the coronation stone of Scotland on which Kings were traditionally acclaimed at Scone in Perthshire. It was ultimately placed in Westminster Abbey from where it was removed in a daring escapade by a band of nationalists in 1950 and brought back to Scotland. Eventually the Stone was recovered and returned to Westminster – or was it? You'll find many Scots keen to believe that the Abbey stone is a meticulously constructed fake, a fitting if a long-time-a-coming revenge on the 'Hammer'.

The English over the years inflicted a lot of damage on Edinburgh and her castle, but among all the sieges one dramatic rescue for the Scots stands out. In March 1312 or '13 Sir Thomas Randolph (later Earl of Moray) recaptured the castle for King Robert the Bruce by leading a group of 30 men at night and climbing the rock to catch the watchmen unawares. His daring coup was hailed as another success in the War of Independence which was to culminate in glorious victory on the field of Bannockburn in 1314. The triumphant King Robert in 1329 gave Edinburgh the charter which recognised Edinburgh as a burgh, and that document survives in the city's archives to this day.

In the interminable battling between the Scots and English the castle was almost like a shuttlecock, passing into one country's hands and then the other's. From 1335 to 1341 it was the turn of the English, but it was a hollow prize to hold, apart from its psychological advantage. In an exchange between the incoming and outgoing wardens in 1335, it is noted: 'There is no dwelling (habitacoun) within said castle, save a chapel a little unroofed, except about a quarter'. And indeed the site appears to have been let for grazing, as the hill was supposed to give the Sheriff of Edinburgh a revenue. Shades of a recent proposal by a city councillor to allow animals to graze on the grass slopes below the Esplanade.

King Edward in 1336 ordered his English garrison to refortify the castle. John of Kilburn was master mason for the project, William of Swaledale the master carpenter; windows for St Margaret's Chapel were made by Master John, the glazier. It seems that a wall of stone then enclosed scattered buildings of wood, wattle-and-daub or turf, with board, thatch or turf roofs.

The castle was further strengthened by succeeding occupants in the political struggles which racked Scotland through the Middle Ages. That tragic heroine of Scots history, Mary Queen of Scots, whose exploits centred more on her palace at Holyrood than the castle, was in her younger days a pawn in the Anglo-Scottish struggle. Although a treaty of marriage between her and the young Prince Edward was arranged in 1543, Cardinal Beaton had it broken, and the Earl of Hertford and an army of Englishmen landed at Leith the following year to lay waste to Edinburgh.

In 1566 Mary bore the child destined to become James VI of Scotland and I of

Pyrotechnic delights over the castle as the annual Glenlivet fireworks concert sends dazzling rockets into a dramatic fall-out watched by literally hundreds of thousands of spectators from vantage points round the city. With music played in Princes Street Gardens synchronised with the fireworks, the concert is a spectacular contribution to the Edinburgh Festival.

Field Marshal Earl Haig, Commander-in-Chief of the British Expeditionary Force in the First World War – a fine equestrian study by G.E. Wade – stands on the Esplanade. For many weeks of the summer the statue is hidden by the tattoo stands.

England, the ultimate uniter of the thrones in 1603. The Royal birth, her courtiers decreed, should be in the castle. Within a year she had been forced to abdicate and the country was engulfed in civil war between the Regent Moray, representing the infant King, and the Queen's party. All this time the castle was being stoutly defended by Kirkcaldy of Grange, its captain. Queen Elizabeth of England felt she had to supply the new regent, now the Earl of Morton, with troops and money and her engineers surveyed the stronghold for an attack which was mounted with cannon strategically placed. Kirkcaldy's garrison were suffering from dissension, wounds and lack of food and water, and he sought to parley. Eventually on May 29, 1573 he surrendered, but within three months Kirkcaldy and his brother James and other supporters were hanged at the cross. A plaque on the Forewall Battery, just before Portcullis Gate, marks Kirkcaldy's fate.

The regency ended five years later and the king and his court had little subsequent use for his castle. Despite James's plea for the fortifications to be restored as protection for his principal 'jowellis', it was many years before improvements and additions were made. More sieges and captures during the Covenanting and Restoration times ensued, and gradually the present shape of the castle was being formed with permanent stone-built structures, towers and ramparts. The last siege was in 1689 when the Duke of Gordon, the captain and constable, sought to hold the castle for the Catholic James VII who had fled to the Continent from England where William of Orange had taken over. After a five-month blockade the only wound caused was to a cow belonging to the lieutenant-governor. But bombardment had taken a heavy toll of the buildings, having caused an estimated £30,000 worth of damage, part of which was made good in 1695.

After the Treaty of Union on January 16, 1707, it is recorded: 'The history of the castle was comparatively uneventful'.

The 'jowellis' which James VI referred to would have included the 'Honours of Scotland' – the regalia of the crown, sceptre and sword of state of Scotland. For many years they lay undiscovered in an old iron-bound oak chest in the castle, until they were traced in 1818 at the instigation of Sir Walter Scott. The regalia are displayed in the castle today – the crown which in its present form is dated to 1540; the sceptre, originally presented by Pope Alexander VI to James IV in 1494 but altered and almost remade in 1556; and the sword presented to James IV by Pope Julius IV in 1507.

They are in the Palace building on the east side of Crown Square. David II started to build a tower house in 1368 for himself in this vicinity and the house was subsequently extended. A great hall was built beside the tower by James I in the 1430s, and his descendant James IV, early in the sixteenth century, built the present Great Hall and developed the Palace site. Further remodelling took place to bring it to its present form, including the removal of a domed roof on the stone turret early last century to allow for its heightening. The castle flag now flies from that raised turret.

The development of the castle over such a long period into what we see today reflects many periods, including the nineteenth and twentieth centuries, and makes it a fascinating place to visit. From the simple beauty of St Margaret's Chapel on the top of the rock to the cold gloomy vaults where prisoners were kept there is a splendid range of history. The vaults were used for that purpose as recently as 1917 when David Kirkwood, one of the 'Red Clydesiders', was interned there.

Prisoners taken in the war against France in the second half of the eighteenth and early nineteenth centuries were held there. Their graffiti can still be seen on the walls, as can a splendid model sailing ship they made to raise funds for extra food and comforts during their enforced stay – it is displayed in the United Services Museum within the castle.

In one of the vaults is the famous siege gun, Mons Meg, made in the 1440s, probably at Mons. It was a gift from the Duke of Burgundy to his nephew-by-marriage, James II, in 1457, and it could hurl a 300lb ball up to two miles, a formidable, if cumbersome, weapon. It was ultimately damaged firing a salute in 1680, and was later taken to the Tower of London. Again Sir Walter Scott was one of those influential in pressing to have it returned to Edinburgh. It stood on the castle ramparts to be clambered over by children of many generations until the weather started to affect its condition and a new home indoors was found for it. A video commentary now outlines its history.

It is interesting to compare the ancient vaults and the military prison built about 1842; two levels of cells with their descriptive captions remind us of the varying levels of barbarity of military punishment, particularly when prison was regarded merely as a holding place before 'proper' punishment. The castle is still an army headquarters with an active military contingent, and sentries close off the Esplanade to visitors in the evening. As you wander round the Argyle, Mill's Mount or Half Moon batteries you see how the guns would dominate the city and make the townsfolk tremble at the thought of huge cannonballs coming their way. Now the only gun fired is the daily (Monday to Saturday) one o'clock gun from the Mill's Mount battery, which looks to the north over Princes Street Gardens.

The General Officer Commanding in Scotland is automatically governor of the castle these days, a symbolic duty, and when he takes office he formally accepts at a ceremony on the Esplanade the keys of the castle. The Esplanade itself was formed by levelling the steep ridge from the castle entry in the mid-eighteenth century, using rubble and waste from building work on the Royal Exchange building in the High Street; ornamental walls were added to the north and south between 1816 and 1820. Although the slope has been greatly evened from earlier times, it still causes problems at the Tattoo when horses in particular are restricted in their pace because of the dangers of slipping. The governor's house is now the officers' mess, although there is still an official residence for the governor himself in part of the building.

The new barracks, hospital, Great Hall, the quaintly named Hawk Hill and Foog's Gate, Crown Square and the Palace all have their own attractions and interests, but for many the most moving place of all is the Scottish National War Memorial, the latest of the buildings round the square. The Memorial stands on the site of the medieval church of St Mary, and the shell of the existing building was erected as a barrack block in 1755.

After the Great War it was decided to erect a suitable memorial to the Scots men *The Castle* and women who had given their lives, and Sir Robert Lorimer drew up plans. The Memorial, a magnificent and solemn place, was opened by the Prince of Wales in 1927. Amidst the cacophany of guided parties of trippers outside, the Memorial is a sanctuary of peace where you can ponder the sacrifices of the Great War and subsequent conflicts, and think too of all those who battled over the ancient rock which so dominates Edinburgh.

CHAPTER 2

T̲HE L̲AWNMARKET

JUST AS you leave the foot of the Esplanade to go down Castlehill, there is a small plaque above a water fountain. It records the spot where witches and wizards were put to a hideous death in the Middle Ages. King James VI was deeply interested in the

The start of the Royal Mile down Castlehill. On the left is one of the city's 'unknown' buildings, a reservoir built originally in 1849 to serve the Old Town. The distinctive Outlook Tower offering a unique view from its camera obscura and Highland Tolbooth steeple provide contrasting styles of architecture.

demon craft and wrote a book on demonology which set the accepted standards for deciding whether people were tainted by the devil.

The King's views earned him the reputation of 'Hammer of the witches' and his infectious enthusiasm earned Edinburgh a dark reputation. It is said more witches were 'worryit' at Castlehill than the rest of Scotland put together — they were strangled and then burned at the stake.

One test was simple. A woman accused of witchcraft, generally an elderly soul, had her thumbs and toes tied together and was then flung into the Nor' Loch. If she floated she was deemed to have proved her guilt, and she faced death at the stake. If she sank, that was proof of innocence, and if she drowned she was completely vindicated although that couldn't have been much consolation to the victim.

From about 1670 prosecution for witchcraft died out, but through the streets of old Edinburgh for many years the superstitions in its wake were fearfully prevalent.

Take Major Weir, for instance, the outwardly good-living and devout officer in the Town Guard. He was regarded as observing a particularly chaste Presbyterian life. We're told he was a tall dark man, with a big nose, clad outdoors in a dark cloak, and always carrying a staff. He lived in the West Bow with his unmarried sister Grizel.

To that house went many to join him in prayer, but all noted he always carried his staff while performing his holy duties. Indeed folk later said that very staff would run a message to the Lawnmarket shops for the Major, or even answer the door. But such rumours gained credence only after Weir's dark secrets came tumbling out when he took ill and started babbling incoherently about his involvement in incest, sorcery and murder.

His confessions so shocked the town that he was imprisoned, tried in April 1670 and sentenced to be strangled and burned at the execution spot between Edinburgh and Leith. His sister was sentenced to be hanged in the Grassmarket for their liaisons with the devil. As the flames burned round the Major his rod was cast alongside him to be consumed by fire.

Had he merely gone mad and his confused rambling been given credence beyond measure, or was the story his sister told at her trial true? Years earlier, she said, a fiery coach came to her brother's door and a stranger invited them to enter it. Whatever happened in the coach, the Major's power was later to lie in his staff, and Grizel herself was to become a witch, like her mother before her.

Whatever the true story, Major Weir's house in the Bow remained uninhabited for the best part of a century. His apparition, in long black cloak, and carrying the staff, was frequently seen flitting down the street. From his empty house at midnight shone lights, and strange sounds were heard; some people even claimed to have seen the Major clamber aboard a headless horse and gallop off 'in a whirlwind of fire'. It was even said a coach drawn by six horses rattled up the Lawnmarket, and thundered

The old Castlehill school building has been turned into a successful tourist attraction by housing the Scotch Whisky Heritage Centre, one of the many recent innovations to provide more entertainment in the Old Town for the visitor. The cobbled roadway has been retained right down the Royal Mile.

down the Bow, stopping at Weir's closemouth for a few minutes before retracing its path – this, said the credulous, was no less than Satan himself bringing back the ghosts of the Major and his sister after a 'leave of absence'. A wonderfully scary story which fed on its time, and a few houses down the Royal Mile still have the reputation of being haunted by a ghost. And as you peer down the closes and wynds off the main street it is easy to see why in the flickering torchlight of the time such events could easily be imagined.

Almost opposite the witches' plaque stands Cannonball house, named after the iron shot embedded in the gable. Tradition says it was fired from the castle and landed in the wall; another tale is that the ball marks the height to which spring water can rise by gravitation; the most likely explanation, however, is that the owner of the house simply had the cannonball placed in the wall for decoration, thus the house's name.

To the north stands a peculiar set of buildings – Ramsay Garden incorporating Ramsay Lodge, built by Allan Ramsay, wig-maker, bookseller, and author of *The Gentle Shepherd*, who died in 1758. The house was spoken of as a goose-pie because of its design, and when the indignant occupant complained to Lord Elibank, he is said to have got the reply: 'Indeed, Allan, when I see you in it, I think the wags not far wrong'.

Just beside those houses stands one of the least recognised buildings on the Royal Mile – the old city reservoir built in 1849. As far back as 1674 water was brought by pipe from springs in the hills to the south into the High Street; before that the citizens depended on pumps and draw wells, several of which stand down the street to this day. The building is being considered as a possible tourist attraction by opening it up.

The Camera Obscura in the Outlook Tower, as we progress down Castlehill, gives the chance of a unique view of the city – an aerial vision from a fixed position as the town bustles on the image thrown by the camera onto a table top. The Tower was bought in 1892 by Patrick Geddes, the legendary and far-sighted town planner and architect who has his own heritage trail down the Royal Mile. The camera obscura has been in place for more than 100 years, and Geddes fitted up 'the world's first sociological laboratory, nucleus of the University of the Future for all neo-technic thinking and teaching and for the future Encylopaedia Civica', but none of this is visible today.

Opposite the tower is Boswell's Close, named after the medical uncle of James Boswell, the biographer of the great Samuel Johnson whose observation on being shown the view from what is now the Esplanade was the renowned comment: 'The noblest prospect which a Scotchman ever sees is the high road that leads him to England'.

Nearby stood the Stripping Close, like so many named after its purpose or use – here those sentenced to be whipped through the town were forced to remove their upper garments before their public punishment 'from the Castle Hill to the Netherbow'. As late as 1822 whipping was still a punishment in the city, three men being thus sentenced on July 31 that year.

This close housed the printing shop for the *Edinburgh Advertiser*, one of the town's newspapers, also owned by the Donaldson family. During the Napoleonic

The Lawnmarket War the fervent James Donaldson instructed his printers to add extra 0's to the figures of the French casualties in battle. He was so carried away by his patriotism that someone estimated at the end of the war he had killed off the entire population of France.

Ramsay Garden with its white painted fronts overlooks Princes Street from its vantage point just off Castlehill. Allan Ramsay, author of *The Gentle Shepherd*, built his lodge here, and from its shape it was known as the goose-pie. Sir Patrick Geddes planned the other houses round the original lodge.

Towering over this part of the town is the magnificent 241-foot-high steeple of the
former Highland-Tolbooth Church, now being transformed into a visitor centre for
Edinburgh by the same organisation who so successfully developed the Yorvik centre
in York.

The building, foundation stone laid in 1842, was for many years the annual meeting place of the General Assembly of the Church of Scotland, before they moved a
few yards across the street into what is now called the Assembly Hall, fronting the
Mound. This building is on the site of the house occupied by Mary of Guise, the
mother of Mary Queen of Scots, and widow of King James V. She could not occupy
Holyroodhouse which had been burned by the marauding English, and so set up her
'palace' here.

On the north side of the Lawnmarket, 'the chief quarter for persons of distinction,' as it was once described, stand two blocks of special interest. Mylne's Court, a
beautifully restored square for university residences, was built by the King's Master
Mason Robert Mylne in one of the earliest housing improvement schemes. In the
seventeenth century he removed earlier houses to form the square.

James' Court is another example of town improvement by James Brownhill,
originally formed to replace again much older buildings in 1725-27. Here Boswell
had two floors and entertained Johnson in 'very handsome and spacious rooms,
level with the ground at one side of the house, and on the other four stories high'
– indicating how steeply the ground sloped to the north.

It is by wandering into these courts that even now the sense of teeming life in the
old high tenements can be felt. Just a few yards further down, however, is possibly
the domestic gem of the entire Royal Mile – Gladstone's Land, now owned by the
National Trust for Scotland and accurately restored to its original state when taken
over in 1631 by Thomas Glaidstanes, a wealthy burgess.

It is the last building in Edinburgh with its original arcaded front, and the pig in
its pen is a reminder that such an animal would be a common sight in the seventeenth
century. The arcade was a development from the overhanging timbered galleries
which were a feature of many medieval houses. When these galleries came to
be rebuilt in stone and lime, from the end of the sixteenth century onwards,
the proprietors had to preserve the passageway below the galleries and the new
stone fronts rested on arcades, allowing pedestrian access. Glaidstanes replaced the
wooden gallery of his 'land' – or tenement – with the present stone one and built the
arcade.

Gladstone's Land is open during the summer months and well worth a visit to see
a wealthy family's living quarters. The painted ceilings are a particularly interesting
feature, a style of internal decoration much favoured in buildings of that period.

No, despite its appearance it's not a cat. This figure atop a Ramsay Garden roof was originally that of the devil, but Edinburgh's rain and wind have weathered the original shape to make it look like a feline.

THIS FOUNTAIN, DESIGNED BY JOHN DUNCAN, R.S.A. IS NEAR THE SITE ON WHICH MANY WITCHES WERE BURNED AT THE STAKE. THE WICKED HEAD AND SERENE HEAD SIGNIFY THAT SOME USED THEIR EXCEPTIONAL KNOWLEDGE FOR EVIL PURPOSES WHILE OTHERS WERE MISUNDERSTOOD AND WISHED THEIR KIND NOTHING BUT GOOD. THE SERPENT HAS THE DUAL SIGNIFICANCE OF EVIL AND OF WISDOM. THE FOXGLOVE SPRAY FURTHER EMPHASISES THE DUAL PURPOSE OF MANY COMMON OBJECTS.

The reign of cruel persecution of witches in Scotland is recalled by this little fountain at the foot of the castle esplanade. More people, often unjustly accused, died at Castle Hill as witches than in the rest of Scotland in the superstitious 17th century.

While the Gladstanes might have lived comfortably for their period, there were constant reminders that the Old Town was a violent place and death could come suddenly apart from plague or other illnesses which periodically swept through the streets. Just across the Lawnmarket lived Bailie John McMorran, a magistrate of the city and a merchant. He was sent on official duty to inquire into the behaviour of rebellious pupils at the old High School – they were protesting about the reduction of their holidays and had barricaded themselves in. This happened fairly regularly and the Town Council had to negotiate some sort of settlement.

The Rector Hercules Rollock tried unsuccessfully that September day in 1595 to talk his pupils out of their protest, and then appealed to the council for help. Bailie McMorran arrived with a force of city officers. The boys had laid in a stock of weapons and supplies, and warned the bold bailie that they would shoot him if he tried to break down the door – the usual way of ending sit-ins. The bailie thought the warning an empty threat and pressed on. A shot rang out and he fell to the ground, mortally wounded in the head.

The ringleader William Sinclair, who had fired the shot, and seven other scholars were taken to prison as the shocked pupils surrendered. Sinclair was the son of the powerful Chancellor of Caithness and other pupils at the Schola Regia had noble families behind them.

King James VI was consulted at his palace in Linlithgow, and for him it was a delicate problem. There does not seem to have been a trial and the boys, all under 14, were acquitted 'by His Majesty's expres warrand'. It's an interesting aftermath that to this day the rules of the Royal High School still state: 'No gunpowder, fireworks or firearms of any description are permitted to be brought within the grounds, under penalty of confiscation, and such punishment as may be necessary . . .'

Like many closes, McMorran's changed its name, and is known now as Riddle's Close. Across the courtyard was Major Weir's land, with its access from the West Bow at the head of the Lawnmarket. Another rogue frequented the closes and wynds of the Lawnmarket, a character who is said to have inspired Robert Louis Stevenson, a native son, to write his story of Dr Jekyll and Mr Hyde – respectable citizen who assumed a role of irresponsibility and crime by night. His model was Deacon William Brodie, whose father Francis named Brodie's Close. He was a wright, glass grinder and burgess, and for a while he worked in partnership with his son. But for William the prospect of life in respectable society seemed not exciting enough. He was to be found among the throng pressing round the cockfighting pits in dark cellars, betting on the outcome of the bloody fights. And he had at least two mistresses, both of whom bore him a family, so the need for money was obvious.

A skilled craftsman, he hit on a simple plan. It was customary in the 1780s for shopkeepers to hang their keys on a nail at the back of the door or in some other obvious

The Old Bowhead, the name given to the lovely old buildings which marked the junction of the original West Bow and the Lawnmarket. 'Nothing in the Old Town was more picturesque or more characteristic than this group,' says one commentator. They were demolished in 1878 to make way for 'improvements.'

A lovers' tryst in Princes Street Gardens. Here was the Nor' Loch where witches were drowned. King James II had the loch formed as a northern defence for his city, and it extended from the castle rock to the line of the Netherbow. The last part of the loch was finally drained about 1821.

23

The Lawnmarket

The dramatic 74 metre high steeple of the Highland-Tolbooth soars over the entrance to the Assembly Hall. The church was built to serve a congregation and as the meeting hall of the General Assembly of the Church of Scotland. Now the Assembly meet in the hall on the Mound and the old church is being transformed into a visitor centre.

position. Brodie would contrive to take an impression of the key in putty or clay hidden in his hand. His accomplice George Smith, a blacksmith, made replicas of the keys from the mould. Thus the honoured Deacon at night gained entry to many of his fellow tradesmen's premises and removed whatever he fancied. The Brodie gang went

The Fathers and Brethren of the Church of Scotland meet at the General Assembly in the city every year in May. Presided over by their Moderator, the Commissioners discuss a wide range of subjects affecting Kirk members and matters of pressing political and contemporary importance.

Lady Stair's House, off the Lawnmarket, is now a city museum, featuring Robert Burns, Robert Louis Stevenson and Sir Walter Scott. Lady Stair died in 1731, but the initials on the lintel are dated 1622 and indicate that the house was originally built by Sir William Gray, a wealthy merchant.

undetected for several years, but after a particularly daring raid on the Excise office in the Canongate, when he was recognised, he fled the town, and was eventually traced to Amsterdam where he was arrested. He was brought to trial with his accomplice Smith and another of his gang, John Brown, who turned King's evidence, and the full shocking story of the town councillor's debauchery and deceit was unfolded before the High Court. Despite an eloquent plea from one of the leading advocates at the bar, Henry Erskine, Brodie, along with Smith, was found guilty and both were sentenced to death.

Confined in the Old Tolbooth prison to await his end, Brodie apparently remained in high spirits, dressing in a black silk suit and cutting a figure of charm and cheerfulness to his visitors. Ironically Brodie had been asked to make improvements to the gibbet used for public executions. He substituted the drop platform for the ancient practice of the double ladder, and as he was led out on October 1, 1788 he is said to have cast his professional eye over the gibbet and smiled his satisfaction. It certainly worked, and Brodie dropped neatly into the city's history.

There are other tales that Brodie had bribed the executioner to let him wear a steel collar under the noose to prevent strangulation, and that after the execution his body was quickly wheeled away along the cobbled street in an effort to jerk him back to life – but to no avail. His name lives on in the close, and public houses have found him a popular character to be named after in one way or another.

Behind the north frontage of the Lawnmarket – it was originally the Landmarket derived from the produce of the land sold there – is another open court in which stands Lady Stair's House, now a museum. The close and houses are named after the Dowager Lady Stair who died in 1731, and the house was eventually purchased in 1895 and presented to the city in 1907. But like so many of the older buildings it can be somewhat confusing to find the letters WG and GS with the date 1622 carved on the lintel above the doorway. These are the initials of Sir William Gray and his wife Egidia or Geida Smith, sister of a Lord Provost. Thus it would appear that the house was built by Sir William, a prosperous merchant, and when he died the close was known as Lady Gray's Close.

Investigating the closes, one often finds many changes of name before arriving at that used today, many of them simply the last family to hold the property before it was grossly sub-divided or 'modernised' in some eighteenth or nineteenth-century improvement scheme. Other closes were simply swept away as new buildings or streets came along, and their location can be traced only on an old city map.

The construction of George IV Bridge and the head of the Mound at Bank Street saw the disappearance of a number of such closes, including Libberton's Wynd, which can be traced by name as far back as 1474. Here the celebrated John Dowie had a

A cyclops eye peers along George IV Bridge from beneath the dome of the Bank of Scotland headquarters. The original building dates to 1802-6 and it was subsequently extended and altered some 60 years later. The bank museum is sited in the building.

tavern to which flocked the merry crowd looking for a night of entertainment in its tiny rooms. One of the specialities of the maison, apart from the flowing drink and the inevitable oysters, was 'Nor' Loch trout' – a fancy name for a plate of haddock fried with breadcrumbs and butter.

Also demolished was the eighteenth-century property of the Baxters or Bakers, where Scotland's bard Robert Burns stayed in Edinburgh in 1786. Bank Street leads to the magnificent head office of the Bank of Scotland, originally built in 1806 but substantially improved by 1870 into one of the finest-looking buildings on the Old Town skyline.

ST GILES TO THE TRON

CHAPTER *3*

*W*HEN YOU step across the junction of the Lawnmarket and George IV Bridge, just beside the old well and opposite the main Sheriff Court building is the site of the last public execution in the High Street. These were truly popular events and the better known, or even admired, the criminal, the greater the crowds.

A few yards further down the Royal Mile, just past the bronze statue to the fifth Duke of Buccleuch, is the 'Heart of Midlothian', the granite setts in the shape of a heart into which a disgusting custom encourages the local citizenry to spit as a sign of good luck. Brass plates on the roadway also indicate the position of the building which in its lifetime from as far back as the fifteenth century served as a meeting place for the Scottish Parliaments, the town council and law courts. It was also a prison and place of execution, it was the dreaded Old Tolbooth.

'At the north-west corner of St Giles's Church, and almost in the very centre of a crowded street, stood this tall, narrow, antique, and gloomy-looking pile, with its black stanchioned windows opening through its dingy walls, like the aperture of a hearse, and having its western gable penetrated by a hole which occasionally served for the projection of gallows,' wrote historian Robert Chambers.

It stood five storeys high and before it was demolished in 1817 had a leading role in the town's life. In its latter days a private of the town guard 'always paraded, or rather loitered, with his rusty red clothes, and Lochaber axe or musket'. The building also contained a hall which served as a chapel, with a spectacular pulpit from which prisoners were frequently harangued for their sins by visiting ministers.

Its origins stretched as far back as 1438 when there is note of a town house or tolbooth, and during the reigns of King James II, III, IV and V the Scots Parliament met in the 'tolbooth'. It appears to have been rebuilt about 1500 and the Court of Session met in the presence of the King there on May 27, 1532; both Parliament and the council shared the premises. It also began to be used as a prison, like tolbooths throughout Scotland, and on occasion the heads of executed prisoners were displayed as proof of the final sentence and as a warning to would-be troublemakers.

When the Tolbooth, such a familiar sight in the town, was finally demolished in 1817, its gateway with door and padlock was re-erected at Sir Walter Scott's home at Abbotsford, an appropriate resting place for a remnant from what he named the 'Heart of Midlothian'. The Tolbooth's gruesome cage was bought by the council of

(*Right*) St Giles from the north-west as it was before 1827. The poet Robert Fergusson's 'air-cock' is still atop the crown spire, but the clock faces have long since gone. The church is open daily to visitors and provides a haven from the bustling High Street.

(*Above*) The Heart of Midlothian. The Old Tolbooth was taken down in 1817. A heart-shaped stone on the High Street marks the site of the building, which also served as a meeting place for Scottish Parliaments and for the town council and law courts.

Portobello as a prison. The Tolbooth had no favourites, and while a few did escape, for many it was a last resting place before execution; for others it was debt which kept them in the terrible conditions behind its walls.

The liberal-minded advocate and author of *The History of Edinburgh*, Hugo Arnot, writing in 1788, describes the Tolbooth as being kept in a 'slovenly condition', with one quarter particularly intolerable. In the 'iron room' destined for those who had received the death sentence, he found three boys – 'one of them might have been about fourteen, the others were about twelve years of age. They had been confined about three weeks for thievish practices'.

The neighbouring St Giles was the first parish church in Edinburgh after the Reformation, and retained the name of the town's patron saint despite the mob throwing into the Nor' Loch in 1557 an image of St Giles taken from the church, and what is said to have been his arm bone resting on a silver mount.

A famous incident took place on July 23, 1637 when, on the introduction of the new Episcopal prayer book, Jenny Geddes threw her stool at the dean who read from it. She was a herb seller with a stance at the Tron Kirk, and her action sparked off riots in the streets. St Giles was only briefly a cathedral, during an Episcopalian phase in the seventeenth century, and correctly is the High Kirk of Edinburgh. Its distinctive crown spire and tower are surrounded by a nineteenth-century building, following the restoration of 1829. A church building has stood on the site for more than 800 years.

John Knox, the first minister of the Reformed faith in the city, bellowed his message from the pulpit, latterly having to be lifted by two servants into it, but once there 'he was sa active and vigorous that he was lyk to ding that pulpit in blads, and fly out of it'.

It was King Charles I who in 1633 made Edinburgh an Episcopal see and ordered the council to convert St Giles into a cathedral 'as is decent and fitte for a Churche of the Eminencie'.

Episcopacy was short-lived, being abolished by the Church of Scotland's General Assembly in 1638. Although Charles II briefly revived the cathedral scheme, plans to remodel the church into a cathedral proper were not realised. For many years the interior was partitioned, allowing the High Court, West St Giles, and the Old Church congregations to worship there until in 1883 the whole interior was opened into one church.

Intensive work has been going on in recent years to restore the church once again, and the cockerel on top of the crown (built about 1500) was regilded and replaced – the sight that Edinburgh's poetic genius Robert Fergusson recalls: 'Now morn, with bonny Purpie-smiles, kisses the Air-cock o' St Giles'.

The church has a special place in Scotland's national life, being the centre of royal and civic ceremonial.

John Knox himself was interred in the old burying ground now turned into a car park between the church and the Court of Session, and the brass letters I.K. on the ground mark his resting place.

This century the magnificent Thistle Chapel designed by Sir Robert Lorimer was added to St Giles', and here the monarch installs the Knights of Scotland's Most Ancient and Most Noble Order in their distinctive green cloaks and caps. Their number is restricted to 16, excluding the Royal Knights, all distinguished Scotsmen. The Queen Mother, who has a special place in Scottish hearts, is Lady of the Thistle and the Queen is Sovereign of the Order.

Although operating as a church, St Giles is open daily to visitors, many finding within a haven of peace from the bustle of the High Street. There are many fine features inside, too, not least the stained-glass windows.

The old Mercat Cross is in the forefront of this sketch which shows the Luckenbooths up against St Giles. Between the Luckenbooths, ripped down in 1817, and the church ran the Krames, a narrow passageway packed with peddlars plying their wares.

St Giles to the Tron

The Mercat Cross rebuilt in 1885 by William Ewart Gladstone, the Liberal Prime Minister, now stands outside the east doorway of St Giles. Royal proclamations are made from the cross by the Lord Lyon, King of Arms, attended by members of his court.

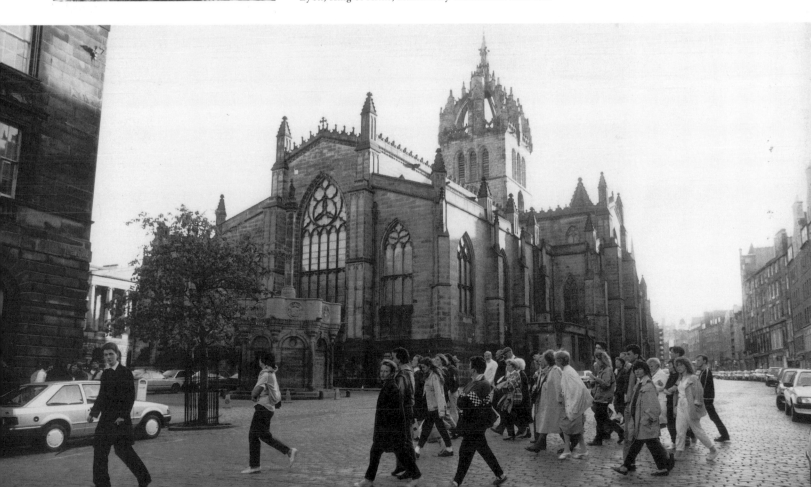

St Giles to the Tron

The beautiful stained-glass windows of St Giles are greatly admired. And another highlight of the building is the Thistle Chapel, designed by Sir Robert Lorimer, which was added to the church this century.

John Knox, the fiery preacher, stands in St Giles, where he was minister. The Reformer was first minister of his faith in the city and preached to the last, even having to be lifted into his pulpit.

Close by St Giles stood the Luckenbooths, a row of shops in a four-storey timber-fronted tenement which narrowed the street to about 15 feet on its north side. The Luckenbooths were taken down in 1817, many famous citizens having enjoyed their use.

Allan Ramsay moved in about 1726 to set up the first circulating library from his first floor in the Luckenbooths. Sixty years later Ramsay's premises were used by the publishers Alexander Kincaid and William Creech, each in turn Lord Provost. Creech himself published many booklets including a topical piece on life in the city in the late eighteenth century, and he was also Burns's publisher.

Between the Luckenbooths and St Giles was a narrow passageway called the Krames (or Creams); it was packed with traders plying their wares from little pitches – gloves, toys, lollipops, says Robert Chambers. 'It was like one of the Arabian Nights' bazaars in Bagdad,' says Lord Cockburn, the judge who wrote so much about the city's life. 'Throughout the whole year it was an enchantment. Let any one fancy what it was about the New Year, when every child had got its handsel, and every farthing of every handsel was spent there. The Krames was a paradise of childhood.' Traders used the place from around 1550 until the Krames too vanished in 1817.

Much of the Old Town's gossip and business centred round the old Mercat Cross, not the one now at the back door of St Giles. That was erected only in 1885 by the Prime Minister, William Ewart Gladstone, who represented the Midlothian constituency. The shaft is believed to be from the original cross whose site is marked close by with brass studs, and it was round this cross, said Mr Amyat, King's Chymist, 'a most sensible and agreeable English gentleman', that in a few minutes he could 'take fifty men of genius and learning by the hand'.

It was primarily a place of trade – the market cross – but because of its central position it also served as a place for barbarous executions and punishments over the centuries. It was a centre for entertainment and rejoicing, a rallying point for the populace. There is a record of the cross from 1365 and it has had various sites in the High Street. It is still part of the city's ongoing history that proclamations such as a Coronation or the Dissolution of Parliament are made from the cross days after they are made in London – it took time for a messenger to travel north in olden times with the news.

As the merchants gathered round the cross in the eighteenth century their talk more frequently turned to the need for a proper exchange building. Although the city's main streets were broad, they were encroached on by the markets, and the closes and wynds were steep, narrow and very dirty. In 1753 plans were drawn up of an exchange building and old property on the north side of the street was acquired by the council and cleared away. John and Robert Adam were the architects and the

There is always the chance of catching a glimpse of ceremonial in Edinburgh. Here Scotland's judges (*above*) process from Parliament House to St Giles for the annual kirking which marks the start of the law term. Their mace-bearers lead the way.

Members of the Most Ancient and Most Noble Order of the Thistle parade in their finery for a service in their chapel, but the highest in the land seem to be making little impression on one passer-by. Membership is restricted to 16 knights, excluding the royal knights, and the Queen is Sovereign of the Order.

building was duly completed. But despite the talk the merchants preferred to gather round the statue of Charles II behind St Giles and did not move into the Exchange, which was eventually taken over as the headquarters for the various departments of the Corporation. The District Council continue to use it as the City Chambers.

One of the most fascinating features is that you can still walk down one of the old closes covered by the City Chambers building; it was encased in the building of the Exchange, and shops and other apartments are still there, remnants of Mary King's Close which acquired a reputation of being haunted after a bout of plague hit the town and it was abandoned about the middle of the seventeenth century.

The Charles II statue – described by a contemporary writer as 'formed in the Roman manner, like one of the Caesars, almost naked and so without spurs and without stirrups' – is a splendid lead figure of the monarch on horseback, and well worth comparison with the statue of Bucephalus in the City Chambers courtyard.

King Charles stands in Parliament Square, outside the Parliament House completed in 1641, and Parliament Hall itself is at ground level with the Laigh Hall underneath. The House is now incorporated into the principal court buildings for Scotland, the High Court which deals with criminal law, and the Court of Session which handles civil disputes. Wigged and gowned as they await court call, advocates stride up and down under Parliament Hall's fine hammerbeam roof in earnest conversation.

It was in Parliament Hall that the decision was taken in 1707 to vote for the Act of Union with England and end Scotland's own independence. The issue caused bitter debate and controversy at the time, many who voted for Union had been bribed, and strong Scottish nationalist feelings continue to this day. 'There's an end to an auld sang' is said to have been the remark of the Earl of Seafield at the dissolution of the last Scottish Parliament on 28 April 1707. Parliament House then became the Court of Session. Its independent judicial system is still one of the features of Scottish life, giving our advocates a good living in higher and lower Courts.

If Deacon Brodie was the inspiration for Stevenson's Jekyll and Hyde, then he found in Lord Braxfield the inspiration for his judge, Weir of Hermiston. Braxfield is described by Cockburn as 'the giant of the bench' in the latter years of the eighteenth century. 'Strong built and dark, with rough eyebrows, powerful eyes, threatening lips, and a low growling voice, he was like a formidable blacksmith. His accent and his dialect were exaggerated Scotch; his language, like his thoughts, short, strong and conclusive.'

His barbed remarks sent advocates scurrying for cover, and he is reputed to have enjoyed teasing a prisoner before sending him to Botany Bay or to the gallows with some final insult. He once told an eloquent 'panell' (as the accused in Scotland was formerly called) who had made an impassioned plea on his own behalf: 'Ye're a vera clever chiel, man, but ye wad be nane the waur o' a hanging.' Braxfield died in 1799 in his seventy-eighth year. Cockburn could write 40 years later: 'His name makes people start yet.'

In those days criminal trials generally went on into the evening or night until they were finished, and the judges openly swilled claret or port at the bench as they heard the cases. A hard head was a necessity.

Cockburn, again, about Lord Hermand: 'No carouse ever injured his health, for he was never ill, or impaired his taste for home and quiet, or muddled his head; he slept the sounder for it, and rose the earlier and the cooler. The cordiality inspired by claret and punch was felt by him as so congenial to all right thinking, that he was confident that he could convert the Pope if he could only get him to sup with him. And certainly his Holiness would have been hard to persuade, if he could have withstood Hermand about the middle of his second tumbler.'

Nor must we forget another judge noted for his peculiarities. Lord Gardenstone, who died in 1793, had a predilection for pigs. He became so attached to one that it followed him round like a dog and slept in the same bed as its master. When the animal grew to full size, his Lordship was unwilling to send his friend to the butcher's but allowed it to sleep on his clothes which he laid on the floor for it. Lord Gardenstone said the pig made his clothes warm for the morning – and doubtless the smell mingled with all the others in a stinking, crowded town, and was barely noticed. Now the judges are generally much better behaved, and you can still see many of them stroll, bowler-hatted and stripe-trousered, up the Mound from their New Town homes to the courts.

As might be imagined in a town of packed lands, many of them wood, the threat of fire was always present. In 1824, Chambers, probably the Old Town's most prolific historian, and founder with his brother of the distinguished printing and publishing house, says the year 'has been remarkable, beyond all former years, for the number of its fires; one each month being the lowest calculation'.

But worse was to come. The 'great fire' of Edinburgh broke out on Monday November 15, 1824 at a little before ten o'clock at night. Smoke was billowing into the High Street from the second floor of a house at the head of Old Assembly Close occupied by copper plate printers. Fire engines and their crews and soldiers from the Castle were called as the Lord Provost, magistrates and the Sheriff sought to direct operations, but because of the narrowness of the close the fire engines could not gain access and very quickly – by midnight – the flames spread from house to house until three tenements were 'involved in one tremendous blaze'.

Chambers records in his eye-witness account: 'While the three front tenements were yielding to destruction the night was calm and serene, and the sparks sent by the flames rose into the air, like embers shot from the crater of a volcano.' Chimneys were set on fire and the Tron Kirk was enveloped by the sparks, without any apparent

This magnificent coat of arms marks where the Scottish Exchange operated from after the great fire of 1824 which required the rebuilding of much of Parliament Square. Parliament House itself was undamaged by the fire.

King Charles II sits astride his horse in Parliament Square. The life-size figure is portrayed as a Caesar, and the statue is of lead. It probably came from Holland and was supplied in 1685, and has been restored on several occasions.

danger at this time. In a rising wind, however, the fire was spreading down the High Street and back tenements were also blazing. Many old buildings collapsed, but by nine in the morning the fire was at last under control and being subdued.

Then the word spread that the Tron Kirk itself was ablaze.

'This edifice being separated by the breadth of a street from every other building, and at the distance of nearly two hundred yards from the former conflagration, was the last place where the flames might have been expected to revive. Moreover, there was something sacred in its character as a church, which, in everybody's idea, was supposed to exempt it from the attack of any such calamity. In the excitement of the moment, numbers breathed within themselves, or

The hammerbeam roof of Parliament Hall was built about 1640 and for centuries advocates and judges have walked beneath. The walking up and down the hall is part of an advocate's way of life. Here in 1707 the Scottish Parliament decided to accept the Treaty of Union to unite Scotland with England in 1707.

Another fine equestrian statue is in the forecourt of the City Chambers. Bucephalus and Alexander make a fine contrast with Charles II. The Chambers were originally built as the Royal Exchange, and the archways leading into the square contained shops.

half-expressed the belief which they entertained, that it was 'judgement-like!'and even the most unconcerned and profligate persons found themselves incapable of beholding this terrific scene with indifference.'

All effort to save the fine building foundered and the watching crowded sighed in dismay as the spire fell. The firefighters did, however, manage to salvage something of the building, and again it was thought that the fire was finally out.

At ten that Tuesday night, however, a new alarm was raised in Parliament Square 'in the top-storey of that immense pile of building on the south side of the Square, formerly pointed out to strangers as the highest in Edinburgh, being at the back part which overlooked the Cowgate, eleven storeys in height'.

This latest blaze ripped through the building – 'The Parliament Square and St Giles resounded with awful echoes: the torches of the firemen below threw up a horrid

Every close off the Royal Mile has a picture of its own. Here the view down Advocate's Close is across to the New Town and the magnificent Scott Monument, completed in 1846. The spire rises 61 metres and is a remarkable tribute to the author-lawyer who loved his native town. Advocate's Close houses the offices of the Old Town Association (page 145).

light upon the tall surrounding buildings; and as the flames proceeded, volumes of smoke and embers were driven eastward in violent and appalling career across the Old Town.'

The fire continued to rampage and the citizens must have wondered what would finally happen – 'The venerable steeple of St Giles reared itself amidst the bright flames, like a spectre awakened to behold the fall and ruin of the devoted city,' said the *Evening Courant*.

At last James Braidwood, director of engines, who was shortly afterwards to form the first municipal fire brigade in the world as a direct result of the 1824 conflagration, was able to say the fire was out, and the tremendous damage could be assessed – along the High Street, four lands six storeys high; two wooden lands down towards the Cowgate; in Old Assembly Close four lands of six or seven storeys; six smaller tenements in Borthwick's Close; four lands of six storeys in Old Fishmarket Close – all destroyed. And, says Chambers, 'Downwards nearly as far as the Cowgate, nothing was to be seen but the frightful heaps of ruin.'

Along the front of Parliament Square four double lands from seven to eleven storeys were also destroyed. Six persons at least died and as many as 400 families lost their homes. One old woman watching over her rescued furniture at a close head told her neighbour the whole calamity 'was a judgement in consequence of the late music festival' in the town.

The destruction of so much property meant the building of a new range of court buildings in Parliament Square – Parliament House itself was undamaged. The early (lower) Signet Library was also undamaged, and its upper chamber, so frequently used for recitals or receptions, and the Advocates' Library behind the hall were yet to be built.

The rebuilding programme also meant a new frontage for the High Street stretch below St Giles and down to the Tron itself, although many of the closes were retained and still exist.

The Tron's steeple was rebuilt in 1828 to a taller design than the original. The church, which takes its name from the weigh beam (tron) standing outside, was built between 1636-47 to house a congregation made homeless when St Giles became a cathedral. It was subsequently subjected to several alterations before the fire and is now one of the town's most distinguished buildings – from the outside anyway. What its ultimate fate is to be is still uncertain. At one time it was a shell, but recent excavations have unveiled the line of Marlin's Wynd, an ancient alleyway which owes

One of the most magnificent settings in Edinburgh is the Signet Library, which in fact contains two libraries linked by a 'grand triumphal staircase.' Under the ornate ceiling of the Upper Library concerts are performed, and receptions are held. The central saucer dome was painted in 1821 with Apollo and the Muses among the figures.

its name to Walter Merlion, a French mason who first paved the High Street in 1532. He asked to be buried at the wynd mouth. At its foot for many years was the town's pudding market where all kinds of tasty meat morsels were offered by the traders. As one historian puts it of Marlin's: 'The close was first robbed of its head for the Tron Kirk, and finally cleared away for Blair Street, 1788.'

A similar end came to many closes, particularly with the driving through of the major bridges – George IV Bridge and North and South Bridges connecting Old and New Towns. But in the stretches between the two great churches on the south side of the street we have closes which tell us something of their history by their very names – Old Fishmarket, Old Assembly, where the dancing rooms moved about 1720 from the West Bow and were burned out in the great fire; Covenant, built about 1600 originally, but its final name comes from the copy of the National Covenant which lay for signature there by supporters of the Presbyterian cause.

Across the street, Anchor Close, where the Anchor Tavern stood, and where later the printer Smellie produced the first edition of the *Encyclopaedia Britannica*. And there too is the distinctive plaque marking where James Gillespie, he of the snuffman's nose, and his brother ran their little shop, stocked by the snuff produced at their mill on the Water of Leith. Fleshmarket Close led to the flesh market on the northern slope, and Cockburn Street itself, named after the worthy judge whose defence of old buildings in particular is reflected in the name of Edinburgh's amenity group, the Cockburn Association, was carved across the lines of old closes to provide another link between Old and New Town.

It's Hogmanay and the place to welcome in the New Year is the Tron Kirk. As the bells ring out midnight and the celebrations start, the crowd raise their glasses and join in the revelry.

CHAPTER 4

FROM THE TRON TO THE WORLD'S END

THE NORTH and South Bridges destroyed a chunk of the Old Town in their very construction, simply because closes had to be swept away to open up spacious new streets. The South Bridge was thrown across the valley of the Cowgate where only one of its nineteen great arches is visible. The foundation stone of the North Bridge, linking High Street and New Town, was laid in 1763, but it was not finished until 1772. The present bridge is a late nineteenth-century design. South Bridge was built in 1785-8 and was part of a development which included Hunter Square, round the Tron, and Blair Street running down into the Cowgate.

As the Royal Mile continues its run east of the bridges down an increasingly steep slope, the view includes North Berwick Law, the distinctive hill which rises over the East Lothian seaside resort across the bay.

The first close down on the north side, Carruber's, is believed to be called after William Carroberos (or de Carabris), a magistrate in 1454. It is certainly one of the oldest to retain its original name, and during the seventeenth and eighteenth centuries was a stronghold for the Jacobite cause. At the foot of the close stands St Paul's Episcopal Church, founded by Alexander Rose, Bishop of Edinburgh, after the expulsion of the Episcopalians from St Giles in 1689. The congregation worshiped in humble chapels, including a wood store, before the church, which has a Jeffrey Street address, was built on the store's original site in 1883. Among its attractions are the Seabury Chapel, which commemorates Bishop Samuel Seabury, the first Bishop of the American Episcopal Church, who worshipped with the congregation while a medical student in the city. He was consecrated in Scotland in 1784.

Curruber's Close was also the site of a very short-lived attempt by Allan Ramsay senior to launch a theatre. An advertisement in the *Caledonian Mercury* in September, 1736 announced that 'The New Theatre in Carruber's Close, being in great forwardness, will be opened on the 1st of November'. Ramsay offered annual tickets at a subscription fee of 30 shillings – 'after which none will be disposed of under two guineas'. The theatre was brusquely closed by the magistrates. Frustrated as an impresario he might have been, but Ramsay patriotically published from this close collections of Scottish poems, songs amd ballads, and a verse play, *The Gentle Shepherd*.

On the opposite side of the main street runs Niddry Street, named after the wynd

From the Tron to the World's End

The Tron Kirk, standing at the junction with South Bridge, has a question mark hanging over its future use, but it is very much part of the city's skyline and will be preserved. Inside, part of the 16th century Marlin's Wynd has been uncovered and visitors can examine the ancient close. To the left, between Niddry and Blackfriars Street, after many years' indecision, a longstanding gap-site was being filled with a mixed development of hotel, flats and shops when this picture was taken.

49

The stone carving marks the close where in 1861 a tenement collapsed, burying 35 persons. One man trapped by the rubble encouraged his rescuers to 'heave away' as he was still alive. And the phrase was incorporated into a memorial stone: 'Heave awa' chaps, I'm No' Dead Yet'.

which stood under the line of the bridge. It too can be traced back in unaltered name over the centuries to Robert Niddry who was a magistrate in 1437. Its name over the years has varied in spelling, however, depending on the whim of the occupant – Nidery's, Nithrie's and Nethery's.

Below Carruber's Close is Bishop's Close, derived from Bishop's Land which stood there. The problem, as one city historian puts it, is what bishop? There is a view – and this is the line the plaque on the close wall takes – that it is named after Thomas Sydserf, Bishop of Orkney, who produced the *Mercurius Caledonius*, Scotland's first newspaper, in 1661-62. The *Mercurius* lasted a mere ten issues from December 31, 1661 to March 28 the following year, and the original editions can be seen in the National Library of Scotland on George IV Bridge.

One of the minor legends in the city's lore is incorporated in the stone above the entry to Paisley Close. A stately old stone tenement stood at the head of the close on the High Street.

'After standing for close on 250 years, it sank suddenly – and without any premonitory symptoms or warning – to the ground with a terrible crash at

A close mouth and a glimpse
of the garden behind. Bailie
Fyfe was a merchant who
owned property in the area and
was senior bailie on the town
council in 1686. Many of the
closes bear the name of their
former occupants and often a
close changed name with a new
owner.

51

From the Tron to the World's End

Tweeddale Court, and the sense of the height of many of the Royal Mile buildings can be felt by dodging off the main street to see what lies behind the facades. In Tweeddale Court is the Scottish Poetry Library.

One of the many fine buildings swept away in Old Edinburgh — the Trinity College Church which stood on the site needed for the Waverley Station. The building dated from 1460 and panels from the altarpiece are now displayed in the National Gallery at the Mound.

midnight on the 10th of November, 1861, burying in its ruins thirty-five persons, and shooting out into the broad street a mighty heap of rubbish. A few of the inmates almost miraculously escaped destruction from the peculiar way in which some of the strong oak beams and fragments of flooring fell over them; and among those who did so was a lad whose sculptured effigy, as a memorial of the event, now decorates a window of the edifice, with a scroll, whereon are carved the words he was heard uttering piteously to those who were digging out the killed and wounded: Heave awa', lads, I'm no deid yet!'

(*Opposite*) The Netherbow Port was demolished in 1764 to ease traffic congestion – yes, even then Edinburgh had a problem. The narrow gate was one of the principal entrances to the old city, and the clock was incorporated into the Dean Orphanage building in the New Town.

The Museum of Childhood sports one of the many fine signs now decorating the Royal Mile. It is a treasure trove of memories of childhood. Its founder was Patrick Murray, a former councillor who became its first curator.

55

In fact the stone replaces 'lads' with the word 'chaps'.

Slip down Chalmers Close and you will come across a building on which you can clearly see numbered stones. It is the Trinity College Church apse, currently a brass-rubbing centre and all that remains of a fine church which originally stood on the site now covered by the Waverley Station.

When the land was acquired by the North British Railway Company, the then Lord Provost and others concerned about the demolition of such a building thought they had forced the company to agree to rebuild the church on another site. However, after further wrangling it was agreed the railway company should give the Town Council £18,000 to pay for a site and a rebuilding of the church there. The money was handed over in 1848, the church was taken down, and the stones were carefully numbered and set aside on the Calton Hill. Inevitably further argument arose – how could the money be best spent? Where was the best site? Eventually the church was rebuilt in 1871-72 but then a lot of the original stones had vanished and found their way into other projects, the enterprising citizens having their own ideas for their best use.

The Trinity College Church and Hospital were founded by James II's queen, Mary of Gueldres. Work had started in 1460 and its many architectural features included a three-side apse, the second earliest in Scotland. A superb altarpiece by Hugo van der Goes adorned the church, and surviving side panels from it are now displayed in the National Gallery at the Mound. In 1638 the National Covenant was read to the people there, and after the Battle of Dunbar Oliver Cromwell's troops were billeted in the building, causing the usual damage.

One of the city's oldest buildings is Moubray House. Robert Moubray built on the site in 1477, although the current frontage dates from around 1630 and is a variant on Gladstone's Land in the Lawnmarket. Unfortunately so many of the oldest buildings have been arbitrarily swept away, like the Trinity Church Hospital, but when Moubray House was threatened with such a fate in 1910, a public appeal was launched at the instigation of the Cockburn Association to ensure the property was retained and subsequently restored. It is much to the Association's credit that they are still frequently in the forefront of the fight to preserve Edinburgh's heritage, both architectural and scenic.

The neighbouring building to Moubray is John Knox's House. Arguments have raged in learned societies on whether or not the great man occupied this particular building during his ministry at St Giles. Tradition has it that he preached from the windows to the multitude below, and it is a story Edinburgh folk are happy to live with. It is certainly the only house left with timber galleries, once a common feature on the Royal Mile. Again its preservation had to be fought for in 1849 when it was condemned as a 'ruinous fabric and an encumbrance on the street'. The house has some interesting carvings, including the admonition 'Lufe God abufe al and yi

An old well which once supplied this part of the High Street stands just above John Knox's House, the only house left with timbered galleries. The neighbouring building is Moubray House, with the current frontage dating from about 1630.

nychtbour as yi self'. There is also a lovely painted sundial with a carved relief of Moses pointing to the sun hidden in a cloud.

Higher up, on the south side of the High Street, is a new hotel, the excavations for which revealed in 1989 a brief glimpse of very old foundations between Niddry Street and Blackfriars Street. Blackfriars Wynd led formerly to the Monastery of the Black (or Dominican) Friars, founded by King Alexander II, in the Cowgate in 1230.

That section of the High Street which includes the Museum of Childhood – a treasure trove not just for children, incidentally, but for all those who have fond memories of the toys they played with – has been extensively renovated in recent years, bringing back modern housing together with shops. It has been a continuing policy to restore the High Street, providing homes and retaining something of the character of the Old Town.

Tweeddale Court, entered through a narrow gateway, is the site of a mansion built by Dame Margaret Ker, daughter of the Earl of Lothian, which later became the head office of the British Linen Bank. In 1806 William Begbie, a porter, was found stabbed to death in the passageway – he had been carrying upwards of £4000 in notes from the branch in Leith to his head office when he was murdered. It became a *cause célèbre* as every known criminal in town had his lodgings turned over in the search for clues. 'Months rolled on, without eliciting any evidence respecting the murder,' writes Chambers. 'And, like other wonders, it had ceased in a great measure to engage public attention, when, on the 10th of August 1807, a journeyman mason, in company with two other men, passing through the Bellevue grounds in the neighbourhood of the city, found, in a hole in a stone enclosure, by the side of a hedge, a parcel containing a large quantity of bank-notes, bearing the appearance of having been a good while exposed to the weather. After consulting a little, the men carried the package to the sheriff's office, where it was found to contain about £3000 in large notes, those which had been taken from Begbie. The British Linen Bank rewarded the men with two hundred pounds for their honesty; but the circumstance passed without throwing any light on the murder itself.' And so it remains!

The publishers Oliver and Boyd subsequently occupied the old mansion house when the bank moved out, but now it has been converted to flats. Just inside the court, where the Scottish Poetry Library has been formed, is an old shed, said to have been the store for sedan chairs which were carried round by strong Highlanders in the eighteenth and nineteenth centuries.

Arnot relates: 'The street-chairs are to be had on a minute's warning, at all hours of the night or day. The fare is very reasonable; the chairmen are all Highlanders; and they carry the chairs so much better than the Irish chairmen of London, that an inhabitant of Edinburgh who visits the metropolis, can hardly repress his laughter at seeing the aukward hobble of a street-chair in the city of London.'

The quaintly named World's End Close takes its name from its position at the very end of the High Street. One of its other names was Stanfield Close, after Sir James Stanfield of Newmills, East Lothian, who was found dead in a pool near his country house in 1687. His son Philip was subsequently accused of his murder. The times were still superstitious, and it was said that the father's body bled when his son touched it – and this was the dead man's way of identifying his murderer. His servants were tortured to produced the evidence to convict the young Stanfield who met a particularly

The Marx brothers never had it like this. Edinburgh at Festival time is packed with entertainers, many
of whom flood onto the streets to create some publicity. Fringe groups still clamour for every available
hall, while the Fringe Office on the High Street is packed with visitors wanting tickets, souvenirs or the
answers to questions.

gruesome end at the Cross on February 24, 1689. After strangulation his tongue was cut out for cursing his father, his head was spiked on a gateway at Haddington and his mutilated body was hung in chains between Edinburgh and Leith.

Where nowadays the traffic lights mark its intersection with Jeffrey Street and St Mary's Street, the High Street came to an end at the Netherbow Port, one of the city's principal gates. 'Bow' means an arch, and the second Netherbow had a tower and spire. You can still see from the narrowing of the street and the brass studs on the cobbles the tightness of the gate through which travellers had to pass.

In 1764 the Netherbow was pulled down to ease traffic congestion, and the clock which was originally in the tower was incorporated into the handsome Dean Orphanage building in the New Town. It was through the Netherbow that Prince Charlie's Highlanders craftily entered Edinburgh in 1745. When the gate was opened to let coaches out they simply ran through and seized the entrance. From the tower above the gate the dismembered limbs of those who suffered the rough justice of the city were often displayed, dangling in the wind for days as a grim warning to all.

The Netherbow Centre is now run by the Church of Scotland as an arts centre and meeting place, and inside is the bell from the old Port. A sculptured stone panel in the centre's courtyard was also taken from the old gate-house. Dated 1606, it commemorates the marriage of James VI to Anne of Denmark. Sight of the Netherbow must have meant blessed relief to one bunch of characters in old Edinburgh – those being whipped through the town – for it was at the World's End Close up against the Netherbow Port that their punishment, started on Castle Hill, ended, and they could crawl away to nurse their wounds.

Part of the famous Old Town skyline – the upper reach from the spire of the former Highland-Tolbooth Church at the head of the Lawnmarket to the Castle.

A view from the ancient Grassmarket of the Castle, home of St Margaret's Chapel, the Honours of Scotland, Mons Meg, the National War Memorial, the One o' Clock Gun . . . and much else.

Looking up the Royal Mile, this is the view towards the spire of the Tron Kirk from the Canongate. Nearby is the Canongate Kirk, where the Royal Family worship when in residence at Holyrood Palace.

The statue of the legendary Greyfriars Bobby at the junction of George IV Bridge and Candlemaker Row. This is the little dog which faithfully guarded its master's grave in Greyfriars Kirkyard for years after his death.

Dressed like a Roman emperor, King Charles II sits proudly astride his charger in Parliament Square. Behind soars the crown steeple of St Giles. Nearby is the Thistle Chapel.

John Knox's House in the
High Street. Whether or
not the great reformer lived
here, this 16th-century
building with its timbered
galleries is a rare survival.
To the left is one of the
Old Town street wells.

Looking down the Royal Mile past the clock of the Canongate Tolbooth. At the bottom of the long descent is Holyrood Palace. The inn sign to the right refers to the Blue Blanket, the banner of Edinburgh's craftsmen, presented to them by James III.

Holyrood Park. The view up past the ruins of the 15th-century St Anthony's Chapel to Arthur's Seat, from whose 823-ft summit spectacular views in all directions can be obtained.

THE CANONGATE

OUTSIDE the Netherbow lay the burgh of Canongate, one of the separate townships with its own administrative set-up which has been swallowed by a growing Edinburgh.

But first we have to cross the junction of St Mary's Street and Jeffrey Street where they meet the Royal Mile. St Mary's is named after the chapel and convent dedicated to the Virgin Mary, which included a hospital. They were destroyed, probably about 1572. The hospital was at the top of St Mary's Wynd; and in 1522-23 there is noted an annual rent of a booth in the Luckenbooths being sold to the matrons or hospitallers of the Hospital of the Blessed Virgin Mary in Sanct Mary Wynd.

Jeffrey Street was formed under the City Improvement Act of 1867. It started at the west of the head of Leith Wynd (now Cranston Street) which led towards Leith under the Calton Crags 'and occasioned there the demolition of many buildings of remote antiquity'.

The Canongate itself takes its name from the Augustinian canons of Holyrood who were granted a charter in 1128 by King David I to form a burgh between the Abbey of Holyrood and the town of Edinburgh. It remained a separate burgh until 1856.

Writing in 1823, Robert Chambers says: 'As the main avenue from the palace into the city, it has borne upon its pavement the burden of all that was beautiful, all that was gallant, all that has become historically interesting in Scotland for the last six or seven hundred years.'

It was the old approach from the east, and in its time provided town houses for some of the highest citizens, not only in Edinburgh but in the Scottish nation. It has benefited in recent years from rebuilding and modernisation projects which brought many of the buildings back from the verge of demolition to be given a new lease of life as a living area in the city centre.

One of the most catching names as you descend the street is Morocco Land, on the front of which is the half-size figure in stone of a Moor, with turban and necklace. The best story about how the building came to get that name concerns the legend of Andrew Gray who fled from Edinburgh after being condemned to death as a ringleader of riots after Charles I's accession. In 1645 the city was stricken with the plague and scarcely sixty able-bodied men could be mustered to guard it from attack when a Moorish Sallee Rover entered the Forth and dropped anchor off Leith.

The Canongate

The clock of the Canongate Tolbooth, where a long-running exhibition, 'The People's Story', has been set up by the district council, lets visitors know there is plenty of time to explore the Canongate, once a separate burgh which has played an important role in the city's history.

There is a world out there. Dramatic impressions of
life on the Royal Mile can be had from deep inside the
closes, like this one in the Canongate.

Not the Hollywood Bowl, it's the Holyrood Bowl.
From St John's Pend you see that there are houses on
the Royal Mile where people enjoy city centre living.

The little figure on Morocco Land. The almost fairy-tale story of Andrew Gray who came to seek revenge on Edinburgh and found instead love and a wife is enshrined in the statute outside the home he bought in the Canongate after his adventures.

It's peaceful now but the infamous Deacon Brodie and his gang came to grief after their attempt to rob the old Excise Office in Chessel's Court. Brodie, the inspiration for Robert Louis Stevenson's Jekyll and Hyde, was eventually traced to Amsterdam and brought to Edinburgh for trial and execution.

Many famous people lived in the Royal Mile houses where rich and poor, gentry and commoner happily shared a tenement. Adam Smith, author of *The Wealth of Nations*, lived in Panmure House, in the close of the same name, for 12 years, and met his peers at the Cross. He is buried in the Canongate Kirkyard.

A detachment landed and threatened to sack the city. A ransom offered by the magistrates was rejected by the Moors, but Lord Provost Sir John Smith of Groathill went in person to negotiate a sum which was accepted on condition that his son was handed over as a hostage. Smith's only child was a daughter, however, and she was ill with the plague. The leader of the Moors told the Provost he had a remedy to cure sickness and offered to free the city from the ransom if he was not successful in lifting her illness.

She was taken to the Moor's lodgings in a house in the Canongate, and her 'doctor' revealed himself as none other than Andrew Gray. He had been sold into slavery by pirates after fleeing Edinburgh, but won favour with the Emperor of Morocco and was now both rich and famous in that country.

He had vowed to revenge himself on Edinburgh, but recognising the Provost as his uncle and the girl as his cousin, he had taken a gentler tack. The story, of course, has a fairy tale ending. Andrew Gray married the girl and they set up home in the house where the cure was applied. But Gray, who had threatened to return to the city only

From the balcony of Moray House they spat on Montrose as he was paraded through the Canongate and up to his execution at the Cross in Edinburgh two days later. His dignity and bearing silenced many in the crowd who were primed to jeer and humiliate the noble marquis.

66

with sword in hand, kept that vow — he never crossed into Edinburgh, spending his days in the Canongate. The effigy of the Moor is seventeenth century, and Morocco Close is unique in having had no other name.

Across the road lay Stinking Close, a description which speaks for itself! And adjacent was Boyd's Close, after the famous host of the White Horse Inn there, and not to be confused with Whitehorse Close at the foot of the Canongate. Samuel Johnson arrived at the inn to be met by Boswell in August 1773.

There is a tale that James Boyd was a keen backer of horses in the races on Leith Sands, and once when on the brink of financial ruin he put his all on a white horse, which won. Its portrait was put up for the inn sign, and Boyd certainly kept a comfortable house with thirteen bedrooms and stabling for fifty horses.

But when Johnson asked to have his lemonade made sweeter, says Boswell, 'the waiter, with his greasy fingers, lifted a lump of sugar and put it into it. The Doctor, in indignation, threw it out of the window.' The Chessel's Court redevelopment has been one of the most attractive in the street. The court was originally built by Archibald Chessel in the mid-eighteenth century. In the building at the rear of the court was the old Excise Office where Deacon Brodie conducted his last exploit as a housebreaker.

In Playhouse Close was the theatre opened in 1747 by John Ryan of Covent Garden, 'an actor of distinguished merit', says Arnot. It seems to have had mixed fortunes as a playhouse, however, and the shows had to get round the city laws by being a 'concert of musick, with a play between the acts'.

In Ryan's theatre the audiences were wont to show their political feelings, and on the anniversary of Culloden – where Prince Charlie's army was slaughtered by the Duke of Cumberland's well organised military might – in 1749 some English officers in the theatre ordered the orchestra to play the obnoxious (to Scottish ears) tune known as 'Culloden'. But sensing the mood of the audience, the musicians bravely played 'You're welcome, Charlie Stuart'. The military at once drew their swords, and attacked the defenceless musicians and players, but were assailed by the audience with torn-up benches and every missile that could be procured. The officers now attempted to storm the gallery; but the doors were secured.

'They were then vigorously attacked in the rear by the Highland chairmen with their poles, disarmed, and most ignominiously drubbed and expelled; but in consequence of this and other disturbances, bills were put up notifying that no music would be played but such as the management selected.'

The great drama *Douglas*, written by a minister John Home at a time when the church was outspoken against the evil influence of the theatre, was performed there on December 14, 1756, and at its end the immortal (and still repeated) line was hurled from a member of the audience: 'Whaur's your Willie Shakespeare noo?' The opening of the Theatre Royal at the northern corner of North Bridge signalled the end for the Canongate Theatre.

The Masonic Lodge Canongate Kilwinning No 2, where Robert Burns was made poet laureate, has its home in St John's Close. The ring of cobbles on the main street indicates St John's Cross which marked one corner of the temple lands in the Canongate. It was at this cross that several of the Provosts of Edinburgh were knighted, possibly because the city always seems to have owned the land from the Netherbow to the cross on the south side of the Canongate. They gained superiority over the rest of the Canongate in 1636.

The Priory of Scotland of the Order of St John, which exists still, primarily in a charitable role, is in St John's Street where Tobias Smollett, the author of *Humphrey Clinker*, which gives some fine descriptions of life at the time, stayed with his sister in 1766.   Moray House was built in the first part of the seventeenth century – there is no exact date – by Mary, Dowager Countess of Home, as an elegant residence with extensive gardens and orchards to the south. Her elder daughter, Margaret, Countess of Moray, took over the property in 1643 and it remained in the family until 1845. Cromwell stayed there in 1648 and again wintered there after the Battle of Dunbar in September 1650. The Earl of Seafield, the Lord Chancellor of Scotland at the time the Union of Parliaments was being thrashed out, lived there and he and his neighbour, the Duke of Queensberry, the Lord High Commissioner, offered the use of their mansions to supporters of the Union for informal get-togethers and discussions.

From the house's balcony invited guests had a grandstand view to see the Royalist Earl of Montrose, 'bound to the cart with a rope' and driven by the executioner, pass on his way to his death at Edinburgh's cross two days later. His entrance was stage- managed after he had been beaten in battle by the Covenanters on May 18, 1650 at Invercarron, with the aim of humiliating further the noble Marquis. His hands were so tightly bound he could not raise them and he 'looked pale, worn and hollow-eyed, for many of the wounds he had received at Invercarron were yet green and smarting. A single horse drew the hurdle, and thereon sat the executioner of the city, clad in his ghastly and sable livery and wearing his bonnet as a mark of disrespect'. An escort was provided by the city guard, under the command of the notorious Major Weir, the wizard.

The crowd had been primed to shout abuse at Montrose, even to stone him and throw abuse other than verbal at him, but his noble demeanour and natural dignity silenced many.

When Montrose was unbound at the entrance to the Tolbooth, he gave the executioner a gold coin, saying: 'This is your reward, my man, for driving the

This beautiful stone is on Bible Land, built by the Corporation of Cordiners or Shoemakers. The inscriptions come from Psalm 133 and from the Book of Proverbs. Shoemakers' Close is another reminder of the old craft.

Huntly House Museum drumming up visitors. The colourful figures decorate the entrance to the museum which houses a fine local history collection.

The Canongate Tolbooth around 1820. Built originally in 1591 to collect public dues, it was the meeting place of the Canongate Council and served as the local jail Now it is a city museum.

The Canongate

cart.' On May 21 he was hanged at the Cross on a gibbet 30 feet high before being quartered.

Moray House is now part of the College of Education which bears its name. Two quaintly named closes are nearby – Sugarhouse, called after the old sugar refinery to which it led, and Bakehouse, again the natural description for the place where the Incorporation of Bakers of the Canongate had a Bakehouse. It was also known earlier as Hammermen's Close. Beside the close is Huntly House, now a museum,

The Canongate Kirk where the Royal Family frequently worship when they visit Edinburgh. The church was built to house the congregation ordered out of the old Holyrood Abbey by King James VII and is one of the finest buildings in the Old Town. Its yard also provides the last resting place for many famous citizens.

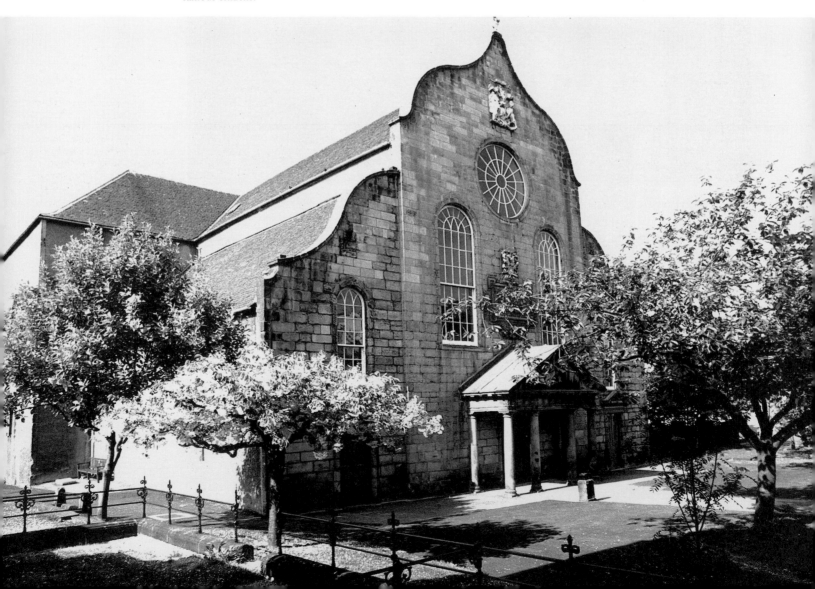

Edinburgh's poet Robert Fergusson died in the Bedlam and was buried in the Canongate Kirkyard in an unmarked plot. It was Robert Burns who recognised his genius and was instrumental in raising a headstone. The grave has subsequently been further enhanced to direct 'Pale Scotia's way to pour her ·r her Poet's Dust.'

erected in 1570 and taking its name from the erroneous suggestion that the first Marquess of Huntly lodged there in 1636. Members of the family did stay there in the mid-eighteenth century.

On the north side stands Shoemakers' Close, named from the Corporation of Cordiners or Shoemakers, and adjacent is Bible Land, also built by the Cordiners in 1677. A sculptured bible is carved above the stair entrance, and a scroll inscribed with the first verse of Psalm 133 reads:

> 'Behold how good a thing it is
> and how becoming well
> together such as brethren
> are in unity to dwell.'

It is followed in smaller letters by a text from the Book of Proverbs – '[it is an] honour for [a man] to cease from strife.'

In Huntly House Museum are displayed many items of local history, including some of the old signs which stood outside city shops. The building was known locally as the 'speaking house' because of the mottoes built into the facade to enlighten passers-by.

The Canongate Tolbooth was built in 1591 originally as a place where public dues or tolls were collected. The council met there for many years, and it was also used as a prison. Now it is another city museum. The distinctive coat of arms of the Burgh of Canongate – with a stag's head and cross – denotes the legendary tale leading to the foundation of Holyrood Abbey and the subsequent settlement of the ownership itself.

King David I was hunting in the then thickly wooded ground we now call Holyrood Park beneath Salisbury Crags when his horse was attacked by a white hart and he was thrown to the ground. As he lay there expecting to be gored by the stag, a silver cloud appeared from which emerged a hand which placed in the King's own trembling hands a sparkling cross. The terrified animal ran off, leaving the shaken king unharmed. That night, sleeping in the Castle, David was visited by a vision of St Andrew, Scotland's patron saint, instructing him to found an abbey on the spot where he had been miraculously saved. Thus the abbey came to be built in 'the little valley between two mountains'— the Crags and the Calton Hill.

The burgh had its own Mercat Cross, which stood in the roadway. But now a cross – its octagonal shaft was provided with a new base in 1888 — stands in the grounds of the Canongate Kirk, which in itself is one of the finest buildings in the Old Town. The parishioners met in the old Holyrood Abbey after the Reformation, but in 1687 James VII ordered that the nave should be converted into a chapel for the Order of the Thistle. The following year the Lord Commissioners of the Treasury asked James Smith to design a new church and instructed the town council of Edinburgh to have it built. It was opened in 1691 as the parish church of the Canongate and its plan is unique among Scottish seventeenth-century churches – a Latin cross with an aisled nave, transepts, chancel and apse.

In the kirkyard are buried many famous Edinburgh citizens: George Drummond, six times Lord Provost and instigator of the New Town and of the Royal Infirmary; Adam Smith, author of *The Wealth of Nations* and father of modern economics; and Dugald Stewart, the philosopher, among them. Robert Burns arranged a headstone to be set over the grave of his fellow poet Robert Fergusson, who died in 1774 in the city's Bedlam, and had previously lain in an unmarked plot. Five years after Fergusson's death Burns wrote the inscription:

'No sculptur'd Marble here nor pompous Lay
No storied Urn nor animated Bust
This simple Stone directs Pale Scotia's way
To pour her Sorrows o'er her Poet's Dust.'

One of the ladies in Burns' life in the city, 'Clarinda' – Mrs Maclehose — is also buried there. They exchanged letters which Sir Walter Scott described as 'the most extraordinary mixture of sense and nonsense, and of love human and divine, that was ever exposed to the eye of the world'.

Close to the church is one of the gems of the Canongate. Step off the pavement through the arch of Dunbar's Close and you are transported back 300 years into a seventeenth century style garden. Laid out much as it would have been in its original state, it's a beautiful reminder that many of the Canongate houses, free from the pressures of the Old Town up the hill, had room for spacious grounds running north and south, offering a gracious life style which could not be offered up the hill in Edinburgh. Here is a haven of peace, a sun-trap, and well worth finding,

One of the finest closes in the Canongate – Bakehouse Close which is named after the bakehouse and property owned there by the Incorporation of Bakers of the Canongate. It was also known as Hammermen's Close.

This doorway is the original entrance from Bakehouse Close to Acheson House, now generally entered from the Canongate. The house now contains the Scottish Craft Centre. The cock crest of the Acheson family and the 1633 date are embellished with the monogram of the initials of Sir Archibald Acheson and his wife Margaret, the original occupants of the town house.

77

if only for a few minutes away from the traffic bustle.

In the close itself stood a celebrated oyster cellar, and when Burns visited he found ladies of fashion wearing masks 'eating oysters and drinking punch and porter'. Such places had a long room where a small group 'might enjoy the exercise of a country dance, to the music of a fiddle, harp or bag-pipe'.

If the innkeeper Boyd had his white horse to thank for his prosperity higher up the Canongate, then skill in another sport certainly set cobbler John Paterson up in some

Whitehorse Close was originally built in the late 1600s round the inn which stood at the far end. There is often confusion between this White Horse Inn and the one which stood at the Canongatehead where Samuel Johnson was met by James Boswell in 1773.

style. When the Duke of York (later King James VII) was staying in Holyrood Palace he was challenged by two English noblemen to a game of golf on the links at Leith. Wanting the best partner possible for this foursome, the Duke was recommended Paterson, a poor shoemaker but 'the worthy descendant of a long line of illustrious golfers'.

The purse was duly won by Duke and commoner (a not unusual pairing in Scottish golf even today) and the delighted Royal Prince handed it all to Paterson. The story goes he was thus able to build a stylish house, Golfers Land, on top of which he placed the Paterson arms – three pelicans, and incorporating a hand grasping a golf club with the motto 'far and sure', the wish of every golfer yet!

Two buildings now catering for the elderly dominate the lower end of the Canongate – Whitefoord House, which is for service veterans, and opposite it Queensberry House, a geriatric hospital. Whitefoord occupies the site of the townhouse of Lord Seton, Provost of Edinburgh, who was host to Queen Mary and Darnley during their honeymoon at Seton. The Whitefoord name is relatively recent, the present property having been designed in 1769 for Sir James Whitefoord.

The seventeenth-century Queensberry House was the residence of the Dukes of Queensberry. During its time it has served as a military barracks, and officers of General Cope's defeated army were held there by Bonnie Prince Charlie's Highlanders after the rout at Prestonpans.

Whitehorse Close was revamped in the 1960s with a new frontage. It was originally built in the late 1600s, round the inn which stood at the far end, and it is likely that the close took its name from the hostelry. Its oldest name, however, was Laurence Ord's after the lands owned by a merchant and his daughter, who kept them until 1695. There is often confusion between this inn and the one at Canongatehead, but in one respect the Whitehorse Close wins hands down – it is one of the most picturesque and most photographed and sketched of all.

At the foot of the Canongate stood the Girth Cross, its site now marked by cobbles. Proclamations were made at this spot and at St John's Cross and it was at the Girth that executions were frequently carried out. Close by on the ground is the letter S – for sanctuary. It marks the boundary of the Abbey Sanctuary, established by King David. Once inside the sanctuary, a man or woman would have the protection of the church.

Throughout its years the Canongate was inevitably linked with the happenings of Edinburgh proper, but it still managed to maintain a strong degree of independence. The street was paved like the High Street and although there was no Provost, bailies, deacons, treasurers, and councillors ran the burgh, its natural protection coming from its links with the Abbey until the monastic superiority was swept away by the Reformation.

CHAPTER 6   HOLYROOD

AS BEFITS a man who has had a vision, King David set about the formation in 1128 of his Abbey with much enthusiasm. His charter granted to the monks of St Augustine was generous in its rewards to ensure that they had both income and influence. Among the endowments were 'the half of the fat, tallow and hides of the slaughter of Edinburgh . . . and all the skins of rams, ewes and lambs of the castle and of Linlithgow which die of my flock; and eight chalders of malt and eight of meal, with thirty cart loads of bush from Liberton; and one of my mills of Dean; and a tithe of the mill of Liberton, and of Dean, and of the new mills of Edinburgh . . .' The charter gave the canons 'leave to establish a burgh between the church and my burgh (Edinburgh)'.

The canons regular were brought from St Andrews in Fife and they lived in a converted nunnery in the castle until the abbey house was ready for occupation about 1176. Enshrined in silver was preserved the miraculous crosss which came into King David's hand, and it remained on the high altar until 1346 when it fell into the hands of the English at the Battle of Durham.

Succeeding sovereigns bestowed more privileges on the Abbey so that it was deemed the most opulent religious foundation in Scotland. Its annual revenues at the Reformation, according to Arnot, were 'four hundred and forty-two bolls of wheat, six hundred and forty bolls of beer, five hundred and sixty bolls of oats, five hundred capons, two dozen of hens, two dozen of salmon, twelve loads of salt, besides a number of swine and about £250 sterling in money'. The site chosen for the Abbey was at the foot of the long slope down from the Castle, and only the ruined nave of the church survives, although exposed foundations of other parts are visible.

The original abbey church was cruciform in plan, but in the latter part of the twelfth century it was rebuilt on a grander scale. Continuing improvements probably went on until the middle of the fourteenth century until the church was complete, and a new chapter house was built about 1400. In 1544 invading English troops burnt and looted the Abbey and three years later the same army stripped lead from the roof. The Abbey was refitted by Charles I for his Scottish coronation in 1633, and it became a Chapel Royal under Charles II. In 1688 the church was stormed by the Presbyterian mob who plundered it, but the principal cause for its now ruined condition was the collapse in 1768 of an over-heavy stone roof. To this day, though, the abbey facade, even in its mutilated state, remains one of the finest early medieval structures in Britain.

The Abbot of Holyrood over the years accommodated royalty, but it is not until 1473 that there is record of some form of permanent royal residence. James IV, however, before his marriage to Margaret Tudor, began in 1501 to have a Palace built in the outer court of the Abbey. Some of the Abbey's own buildings may simply have been repaired and incorporated into the scheme, but a new tower, chapel and gatehouse were certainly built at that time.

A member of the queen's English retinue described the wedding festivities of 1503 and said the dining room was richly dressed in red and blue hangings; the Great Chamber was hung with tapestry representing 'the ystory of Troy tone' while the king's chamber was 'haunged about with the ystory of Hercules togeder with other ystorys'. James IV, with many of his nobility, died on Flodden field in the blackest day in Scotland's history, September 9, 1513, in battle against the English, but the work on the Palace continued. James IV's tower is still at the north-west corner of the present building, but the rest of the sixteenth-century Palace, apart from a fragment of gatehouse, has gone in the wake of several reconstructions.

The entrance gates to the forecourt of Holyrood Palace. The stag with the Holy Rood between its antlers reflects the legendary encounter of King David with the stag while out hunting and his inspiration to start building the Abbey in 1128.

In Scotland the Royal Company of Archers are the Queen's bodyguard, and they are on duty on ceremonial occasions to escort Her Majesty. The Archers became a royal company in 1704 and they still have shoots with their bows and arrows for trophies. They are seen here in the grounds of Holyroodhouse. In the background is the Calton Hill.

The royal garden party is a big social event in Scotland, and when the Queen makes her summer visit to Edinburgh such a gathering is usually held on the lawns of Holyroodhouse. A wide cross-section of society is invited.

King Charles I was interested in extending the Palace but it was his son who, after the Restoration, resolved to rebuild Holyroodhouse. A scheme was approved and under the direction of Robert Mylne, the king's Master Mason, started in 1672. Stone was brought from Dalgety in Fife and from South Queensferry to mingle with the blocks preserved in demolition of the older parts. Paving stones were hewn from a quarry in the surrounding park; marble fireplaces from Italy were shipped from London; the bulk of the finishing timbers and tiles, marble pavings, linseed oil and white lead came from Holland, English glass was used to repair the church windows, but French glass was imported for the Palace itself.

The Royal Family still use the Palace as their base during their annual official visit to Scotland, and the garden parties held on the lawn bring together a cross-section of Scottish society. The Queen's standard flies from the Palace flagpole when she is in residence, as does the banner of any other member of the family staying there at other times, and when in Scotland the Queen's official bodyguard is provided by the Royal Company of Archers. 'This remarkable corps, which takes precedence of all royal guards and troops of line, is composed entirely of nobles and gentlemen of good position, under a captain-general, who is always a peer of the highest rank, with four lieutenants-general, four majors-general, four ensign-generals, sixteen brigadiers, an adjutant and surgeon.'

The Archers became a royal company in 1704 under a charter from Queen Anne although their predecessors had certainly formed a band long before that. In the present day their duties are largely ceremonial and in their dark green uniforms, carrying long bows and arrows, they are never far from the sovereign.

While visitors can see the riches of the Palace in the various apartments, no one can think of Holyrood itself without recollecting the most tragic monarch of all on the Scottish throne, Mary, Queen of Scots. Just after Mary's birth her father James V died at Falkland Palace in Fife, leaving her to face a life of bitter struggle and controversy as the Reformation came to Scotland. They were troubled years and after Mary of Guise, the Queen Regent, died, the 18-year-old Mary came from France to claim her throne in person after thirteen years' absence from her native land. She stepped ashore at Leith and entered the city in 1561, moving into the Palace.

She was serenaded on the first few evenings by 'six or seven hundred citizens who gave her a concert of the vilest fiddles and little rebecs, which are as bad as they can be in that country, and accompanied them with singing psalms, so wretchedly out of tune and concord that nothing could be worse'. That was a Frenchman's view, for she brought a retinue of noblemen from that country with her. John Knox, the fiery Reforming cleric with whom she would clash loud and long, preferred to say: 'They were a company of honest men who with instruments of music gave their salutations at her chamber window'.

The old Abbey suffered at the hands of the Presbyterian mob, but its heavy stone roof collapsed in 1768. James IV started to build a palace in the Abbey grounds in 1501 before his marriage to Margaret Tudor. The Queen always stays in the Palace during her visit to Edinburgh.

In a land where Protestantism was now a lawful religion the teenage Catholic queen ordered the mass to be observed in the Chapel Royal, sparking off a violent protest from the mob when they heard of such a happening.

On July 29, 1565, Mary married her cousin Lord Darnley, who had been created the Duke of Albany, and had pretensions to share the crown with his wife. The queen's secretary was an Italian, David Rizzio, and Darnley, jealous of the man's power, position and influence, and believing him to have turned the queen against the idea of his obtaining the crown matrimonial, became involved in a conspiracy to kill the courtier.

Rizzio was to have been murdered in his own apartments at Holyrood, but the conspirators waited until he was dining with the queen and her guests. Headed by the Earl of Morton, they burst into the chamber and Rizzio was stabbed to death before Mary's eyes. In the frenzy as man after man slashed with his blade at Rizzio's bleeding body, 56 wounds were said to have been inflicted. There is still a stain on the floor outside Mary's apartment, pointed to as the blood of Rizzio.

It was not surprising that early the following year, 1567, Darnley himself was murdered – in a spectacular way. He was staying in the Kirk o' Field when the Earl of Bothwell's men planted gunpowder under his bed and blew the queen's husband to death. The queen herself had attended the sick Darnley in his room the very day of the explosion. The house was destroyed 'even to the very grund-stane,' wrote Mary to her ambassador in France. The bodies of Darnley and his servant were found in a garden outside the town wall, blown there by the explosion. The site is now covered by the Old College of Edinburgh University.

Mary's own involvement in the murder is open to speculation, but she married the Earl of Bothwell only months later in the Great Hall of the Palace. But her stay in Holyrood was to be short-lived thereafter. The nobles revolted against her liaison with Bothwell who fled, leaving Mary to surrender at Carberry, near Musselburgh, and return to Holyrood as a prisoner before her abdication. She escaped from Loch Leven Castle and eventually threw herself on the mercy of her kinswoman Queen Elizabeth of England. She remained a virtual prisoner in England for many years and was eventually brought to trial, accused of being implicated in a plot against the Protestant Good Queen Bess who eventually signed her death warrant.

Mary met her death on the block on February 8, 1587 with a calmness and serenity which affected many who saw her. When the execution was completed and her severed head held high to the cry of 'So perish all Queen Elizabeth's enemies', there was no universal acclaim from the onlookers. She was 44, and she was not to know that her son James VI would become the first monarch to sit on the united throne of Scotland and England in 1603.

Inside the Palace in the 150-feet-long picture gallery hang portraits of more than

Queen Mary's bath house is the traditional name, but in reality it was probably built as a garden pavilion. One commentator, however, even claims that the queen used to bathe in white wine in the building.

100 Scottish kings from Fergus I to James VII, painted by the Flemish artist Jacob de Witt who contracted to execute the work within two years, at an annual salary of £120. How good his imagination was in capturing the likenesses of the earliest monarchs you must judge for yourself, but it is said an awful lot of the portraits have very similar features!

A strange-looking building to the north of the Palace is known as Queen Mary's Bath-house, really a garden pavilion, probably dating from the last quarter of the sixteenth century. But tradition persists that Mary did use it for bathing, one

Holyrood

The Radical Road round
Salisbury Crags provides a
popular walk. Unemployed
weavers were recruited to
construct the pathway last
century. At one time the crags
were quarried before the work
was stopped to prevent further
damage to the rock face.

The last fragments of St Anthony's chapel stand above St Margaret's Loch, and a clamber up the slope provides a fine view of Edinburgh. The chapel dates from the 15th century and was probably built as a hospital for those suffering from skin disease.

commentator going so far as to say she used a bath of white wine to enhance her charms. 'Other no less efficacious means have been assigned as expedients resorted to by Queen Mary for shielding her beauty against the assault of time,' says Sir Daniel Wilson in his *Memorials of Edinburgh*. 'But the existence of a very fine spring of water immediately underneath the earthen floor may lend some probability to her use of the pure and limpid element.'

The Palace and Abbey are set in the Royal Park of Holyrood (or the Queen's or

The new look and the old. If it's all about style, then the majestic style of the palace of Holyroodhouse in the background can fancy its chances against the modern style of the young man.

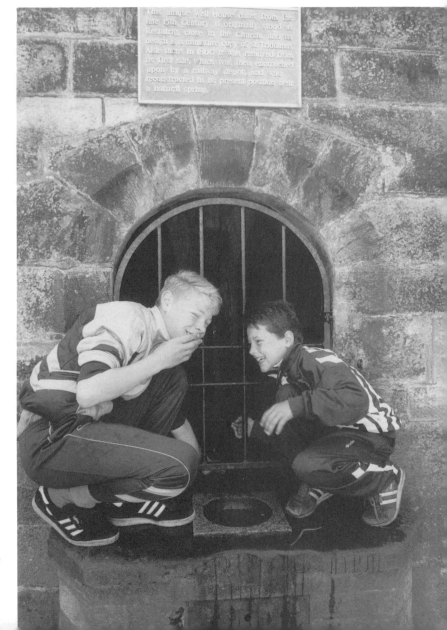

A sip of water from St Margaret's Well which was moved into Holyrood Park from Restalrig in 1859. The water from the original well was believed to have powers of healing, particularly blindness.

King's Park as it is sometimes called). It has covered roughly the same ground since the mid-sixteenth century and is dominated by the 823-feet-high Arthur's Seat, a former volcano whose lion's head and haunch form such a distinctive shape on the city skyline. One Chinese writer thought the outline more like a sleeping elephant. The Radical Road constructed by out-of-work weavers recruited for the task last century lies beneath Salisbury Crags.

Remains of a defensive stone-built rampart run along the upper eastern slopes of Arthur's Seat, above cultivation terraces which can be clearly picked out. There are remnants of four prehistoric forts in all in the park, suggesting it was an area of major importance in the first millennium BC and the early centuries AD. Hut circles are believed to be the earliest monuments in the Park, while there are also signs of home-

Dawn breaks on Arthur's Seat on May Day. Each year the minister of the Canongate Kirk conducts a service on the summit. While some toast the dawn, many young girls wash their faces in the dew in the hope that their skin will remain fresh throughout the year.

steads and enclosures in the terraced area facing Dunsapie fort, with its loch below it. The cultivated terraces are both above and below Queen's Drive and can also be seen in three other places. Terraced strips were originally very narrow ploughed fields.

The Park and its hills offer some splendid views of the town and a clamber up to the top of Arthur's Seat or up the Radical Road is well worth the effort. One ancient custom which is still observed on Arthur's Seat is the May Day celebration of the dawn. A goodly number gather on the hill to watch dawn break, and the minister of the Canongate Kirk leads a short worship at sunrise. Young women wash their faces in the dew in the hope that their skin will remain fresh throughout the year.

On the hill above St Margaret's Loch, the one nearest the Palace, stand the ruins of St Anthony's Chapel. Only part of one wall survives in the building erected in the second half of the fifteenth century probably as a hospital for those afflicted with 'St Anthony's Fire' – erysipelas, the skin disease. The flat ground below has often been used for ceremonial parades, the hills making a natural amphitheatre for those not privileged to have an official entry ticket to the stands specially erected for the occasion.

On the roadway nearby is St Margaret's Well, which was moved from Restalrig in 1859. Its name probably comes from St Margaret whose chapel is at the Castle, and the water from the original well was believed to have healing powers, particularly in the treatment of blindness.

Near the northern entrance to the Park, beside the Duke's Walk, a pile of stones marks the spot where Nichol Muschat of Boghall murdered his wife in 1720. Muschat, a surgeon and 'a debauched and profligate wretch', married his wife, Mistress Hall, within three weeks of meeting. But he quickly tired of her and recruited three accomplices in a plot to rid himself of her. Various schemes failed until the husband, lured by 'the devil, that cunning adversary', as he later confessed, took his wife for a walk in the Park, and cut her throat. He rushed to his brother to tell him what had happened, and ultimately was tried for murder and admitted everything. He was hanged in the Grassmarket, and to mark their horror of the event, townsfolk raised a cairn of stones at the spot where the murder occurred. It was removed in 1789 but restored about fifty years later.

The Cowgate

*T*HE CANONS of Holyrood may have been men of God, but they knew the pleasures which human frailty enjoys – and one of them was good ale. As early as 1200 they had brewed their ale 'in big round vessels which one day probably received the benefit of their laundry and on the next the benison of their beer or rather ale, which in those days was beer without hops'. And so it was no coincidence that in 1778 Archibald Campbell Younger broke away from the family business in Leith to set up his own brewery in the precincts of Holyroodhouse. At this time several hundred people were living in the Abbey confines and ale brewed there did not have to pay the town council tax of two pence on every pint brewed and sold inside the city boundaries.

The view across Surgeons' Square at the rear of the former High School, at the foot of Infirmary Street. The building at the far side of the Square backs onto the Flodden Wall at the foot of the Pleasance. Burke and Hare brought bodies to Dr Knox's anatomy rooms in the square.

There were also many clear springs and wells on the South Back of the Canongate (the Holyrood Road area as it is now known). Brewers naturally had fought any impost as vigorously as they could since the town council of Edinburgh in 1693 had persuaded the Scots Parliament to sanction such a levy, over and above the excise tax. Some of the levy was destined to defray the cost of Charles II's rebuilding of Holyroodhouse, but even this end did not justify the means in the eyes of the town brewers or indeed the consumers.

Younger, however, was one of four brewers who avoided the local tax, and he developed in his ale-house a strong brew which quickly became a favourite at a time when punch and claret were still the popular drinks in the taverns. One of those who pressed the new ale was John Dowie, whom we have already met. In his tavern in Libberton's Wynd customers delighted in Younger's brew – 'A potent fluid which almost glued the lips of the drinker together, and of which few, therefore, could despatch more than a bottle'.

Younger also opened up in Croft-an-righ, and later in the North Back (now Calton Road) on a site merged into the Waverley Station. Eventually the Younger family consolidated their interests under one company, William Younger, and they took advantage of the perfect water in the Canongate Wells, together with the rich barleyfields of Lothian. Thus was founded the empire which was ultimately to become Scottish Brewers with headquarters between the Canongate and Holyrood Road. There the Abbey and Holyrood Breweries produced the amber nectar to quench the thirst of millions of throats throughout the world, and there beer is still produced today although part of the huge site is now being cleared with developing production in other parts of the brewing giant's plants. Two carved stones on a tenement in Holyrood Road, the street which runs from Holyrood Park entrance into the Cowgate, attest to the brewing industry's influence. They are just past Queensberry Lodge, now a nursing home, which was erected behind Queensberry House in 1865 for the 'safe accommodation and reformation of females addicted to the habits of drunkenness'.

On the other side of the street is the area known as Dumbiedykes, tucked in between the Park and the old South Back. Sir Walter Scott suggests that the name came from a house beside the Park, which was so called because an instructor of the deaf and dumb lived there – and that's probably as good an explanation as any.

Holyrood meets, at the junction with St Mary's Street and the Pleasance, the Cowgate where formerly there was a gate in the city wall. But before venturing into another very old part of the town, it is worth turning south and climbing the slope called the Pleasance. On the west side is a remnant of the Flodden Wall, built to strengthen the existing walls after the flower of Scotland was so tragically cut down in battle in 1513, and imminent invasion from England was feared.

Part of the old city wall runs down the Pleasance to the junction of the Cowgate and Holyrood Road. The Flodden Wall was built to strengthen the existing defences after the cream of Scotland was cut down in battle at Flodden Field in 1513.

The dramatic arch of the South Bridge spans the Cowgate, once one of the finest streets where 'the nobility and chief senators' lived. This is the only visible arch of the 19 which support the South Bridge whose construction meant the demolition of many old closes running down to the Cowgate.

The Cowgate   Flodden was a disaster from which the Scots took many years to recover, and the 'News of battle! – news of battle!' as William Aytoun puts it in his dramatic poem was brought to Edinburgh by one of the few survivors, Randolph Murray:

'Spearless hangs a bloody banner
In his weak and drooping hand –
God! can that be Randolph Murray,
Captain of the city band?'

This beer garden in the Cowgate has become a popular summer attraction as the whole area sees a resurgence of housing and a local community. At one time, though, the Cowgate had the worst slums in Edinburgh, and even today many of the down-and-outs find shelter here.

Renovated buildings overlook the close named after the Coinyie or Cunzie House, the Scottish mint which was demolished in 1877. The mint was moved from the outer court of Holyrood during Queen Mary's reign.

Early in the following year the town council imposed a tax to meet the cost of the new wall, and it encompassed the Cowgate and the Grassmarket as well as land to the south of the Cowgate, taking until 1560 to complete. What was called the King's Wall had been authorised in 1450 by James II, and it probably replaced an earlier protective fortification. Between 1628-36 came the Telfer Wall which took in more land bought by the council. There were six main ports, or gates, in both the Flodden and Telfer Walls, with a number of towers. The need for the walls diminished with more settled conditions in the eighteenth century and the town expanded both to the

The Cowgate

Blackfriars Wynd, now Street, in 1837. The narrowness of the streets running from the High Street into the Canongate can be seen, together with the crowding together of animals and people. The crammed buildings and the poor houses last century, however picturesque, created conditions in which illness was rife.

98

north into the New Town and into the countryside to the south. The Pleasance itself lay outside the Flodden Wall, the area taking its name from the convent of St Mary of Placentia which formerly stood there. The Edinburgh tongue corrupted the name to Pleasance. It is worth continuing a few yards further up to slip through the archway of the University buildings on the left to find the old Quaker burying ground with its distinctive headstones.

But back to the Cowgate, the base of the deep gorge into which the closes of the High Street still plunge to the south, and from which rise other closes seeking southern sunlight on the reverse slopes. In its latter days it sheltered the most densely crowded and poorest of the citizens of the Old Town, and when the onlooker peered from South Bridge and George IV Bridge which soared above it the Cowgate seemed to 'cower in its gorge, a still narrow and dusky river of quaint and black architecture'.

At one time it was probably a narrow country path, now it is a vital artery for traffic seeking to avoid the congestion of the streets above. Many timber-fronted houses lined the narrow roadway in the times when 'men of rank superior to any of which modern Edinburgh can boast had their dwellings in the Cowgate, which rapidly became a fashionable and aristocratic quarter, being deemed open and airy'. In 1530, says one historian, the 'nobility and chief senators of the city dwell in the Cowgate'. The name is found at least as early as 1428 and it has also appeared as 'Southgaitt'. Some believe 'Cowgate' means that cows were driven along the road from the meadows outside the wall.

By the nineteenth century it certainly was not the place for the nobility, but a place of downtrodden and illness-riddled humanity many of them of Irish stock. 'The closes are generally narrow, confined and dirty; the "lands" are very high; and the dwellings are for the most part of a wretched description,' wrote a pioneering investigative reporter William Anderson in the *Edinburgh Courant* in a series of articles in 1886-7 destined to draw attention to the plight of the poor in the city.

Of the area bounded by the Cowgate, St Mary's Wynd, the High Street and Niddry Street, he reported: 'This block may be said to be the great centre of the crime, vice and misery of the city,' and his words included this eloquent admonition to his readers:

> 'Much less is known, we venture to say, of the closes of Edinburgh than of many parts of the interior of Africa; and the internal arrangements of the Red Indian wigwam are likely to be much more familiar to the Christian public than is the condition of the hovels in which many of our townspeople live.'

Throughout Anderson's reports runs not only the thread of squalor, but also the abject poverty by which the inhabitants were trapped before various improvement

The spire of the Magdalen
Chapel, seem from Greyfriars
Kirkyard, identifies one of
the Cowgate's least familiar
buildings. Its patrons were the
Hammermen of the city, and
it contains the main surviving
example of pre-Reformation
glass in Scotland.
Overtowering the chapel is the
Public LIbrary on George IV
Bridge.

Another glimpse of the Magdalen Chapel can be caught from George IV Bridge where it passes over the Cowgate. The chapel was founded in the 16th century by Michael Macqueen and his wife Janet Rynd for a chaplain and seven poor men.

schemes helped to lessen their misery. But the Cowgate still, possibly as it is a street with its own unique character, at once public and yet with many hidden nooks and crannies, is a haunt of the down-and-outs, mingling with a student and 'upwardly mobile' population who frequent some of the trendier bars. New housing is bringing another population into the Cowgate, and while it may never attain its former glories, it is definitely on the up and up.

At the east end of the Cowgate is St Patrick's Roman Catholic Church, built in 1772-4 as an Episcopal chapel to serve a fashionable congregation which, however, moved to the New Town. The old High School stands in High School Yards above the Cowgate to the south, at the foot of Infirmary Street. Its immediate successor was the classical Thomas Hamilton Greek Doric structure in Regent Road, set aside at the height of the Scottish Devolution debate to be the seat of the ill-fated Scottish Assembly. Now it houses the Crown Office and occasionally Scottish MP's meet in the Assembly Chamber as a conciliatory gesture. The present-day High School is now on a greenfield site at Barnton.

Running by St Patrick's is South Gray's Close where the Royal Mint of Scotland or Cunzie House stood until its demolition in 1877. It was also, not unnaturally, known as Mint Close. The mint was moved from the outer court of Holyrood Palace during Queen Mary's time to the Castle before the new mint was built in the Cowgate with a date over its 'nobly and heavily moulded doorway' of 1574. Gradually an open quadrangle was formed round the mint where Scottish coins were produced until the Union of 1707. Much of the gold coin was minted from native ore, Parliament granting to the Crown in 1424 all the gold and silver mines. There were variances in the worth of Scottish and English currency. At the time of the Union Scots coin was only one-twelfth the value of sterling, and £100 Scots equalled £8 6s 8d sterling. A £1 Scots equalled 1s 8d sterling (about eight pence in modern terms).

It was in the Cowgate that one of the best-known leaders of the fearsome and fickle Edinburgh mob found his natural place. He was known as Bowed Joseph, a humble cobbler, but he obviously had a dominant personality in excess of his calling and by popular acclaim he was elected by the rabble as their undisputed leader. From Robert Chambers we get this description of the man who could literally hold the town in his hands: 'His person was low and deformed, with the sole good property of great muscular strength in the arms. Yet this wretch, miserable and contemptible as he appeared, might be said to have had, at one time, the command of the Scottish metropolis.'

Bowed Joseph, or General Joseph, Smith was apparently frequently sent for by the magistrates who would consult him at their regular Wednesday morning meetings on their proposals, and they listened and reacted to his views, patronising him 'rather from fear than respect'. When troubles and the crowds became unruly Joseph was

asked for the best means of appeasing them. 'On such occasions nothing could equal The Cowgate
the consequential air which he assumed,' says Chambers.

At the height of his power Bowed Joseph was reckoned to be able to rustle up a
crowd of 10,000 within the hour, beating with his hands a drum which drew supporters from every close he passed. But feared though he might be by the council, Joseph
was always after only one thing, fair play – 'The little man was never known to act in
a bad cause, or in any way to go against the principles of natural justice.' He was very
much a man of the people, much needed in eighteenth-century Edinburgh, and he set
many wrongs to right. His reign ended abruptly in 1780. He had enjoyed a day at the
races on Leith Sands, and having had a good drink was in very high spirits when he
fell from the top of the stage coach bringing him home and was fatally injured. The
council were rid of a troublesome fellow, and the poor folk lost their champion.

The fighting working class is recalled by a small plaque on the George IV Bridge
arch to James Connelly, a Cowgate-born man who was executed by the British in
Dublin for his part in the Irish troubles of 1916.

Standing desolate and awaiting redevelopment just before you reach that arch is Tailors' Hall, built in 1621 and extended upwards in 1757. The Tailors' Corporation had
their charter granted to them in 1531, and had an earlier meeting place in Carruber's
Close off the High Street. Their new hall was opposite the old meal market, and with
its own courtyard and outbuildings it was a popular meeting place. In 1638 when the
National Covenant was taking up many folks' minds, supporters of the Covenant met
in the hall, indeed it became almost an inn for visitors from other parts of Scotland
coming to the capital to seek guidance and information on the document which was
to commit those who signed to an oath in support of the Crown and the Presbyterian
religion.

The draft was read in the 'summer house of the gaird' at Tailors' Hall on February
17, 1638, at a private conference of the Commissioners of the Church of Scotland
Presbyteries, and 'all the Commissioners were of one judgment'. Between 200 and 300
ministers in the hall itself were waiting to discuss the draft Covenant before it got their
approval, and the next day it was signed by the nobles, ministers and commissioners of
burghs in the Greyfriars Church. The hall also served as a playhouse for a number of
years, although it suffered from the competition from the Canongate theatre when it
was opened.

A few yards further west is one of the least known but most significant buildings
in the Old Town – the Magdalene Chapel at No 39 Cowgate. The chapel, which
had a chaplain's lodging and hospital for almsmen, was founded in the first half
of the sixteenth century by Michael Macqueen, a burgess of the city, and his wife
Janet or Jonet Rhynd. The chapel and hospital were designated for a chaplain and
seven poor men, and dedicated in the name of Mary Magdalen. The patrons were the

The Cowgate   Hammermen of the city, a medieval trade incorporation, like the Tailors.

The Hammermen altered the original chapel to serve as their convening hall, and in 1622 replaced the steeple with the present 73-foot-high tower. Above the door is a panel with the initials of Michael Macqueen and Janet Rhynd and the crowned hammer of the Hammermen. The central window contains four sixteenth-century heraldic roundels with the main surviving example of pre-Reformation glass in Scotland. The chapel is now in the care of the Scottish Reformation Society whose office is in George IV Bridge above.

The Hammermen of the city originally included blacksmiths, goldsmiths, lorimers, saddlers, cutlers, buckle-makers and armourers. Pewter-makers and heckle-makers were later included, and they were only one of the many trades incorporations founded to encourage and protect the interests of the old crafts by insisting on training and proper examination in the necessary skills for acceptance to the craft.

The trades incorporations were granted by James III the right to fly a banner or standard, known as the Blue Blanket, which was in the care of the Convener of Trades. It was the rallying point for the tradesmen when called to arms. The original rests in the National Museum in Queen Street, while a seventeenth-century replacement is in the Trades Maiden Hospital in Melville Street.

The Cowgate is one place where it really does pay to look up. From its gorge there are some wonderful sights, the steeple of the Tron for one; there are glimpses of life on the High Street if one looks north up the closes; some of the buildings like the law courts and the National and public libraries soar far above their own street level and tower over the Cowgate.

THE GRASSMARKET

THE GRASSMARKET opens out at the western end of the Cowgate, or the Cowgatehead, and provides a spacious 230-yards-long rectangle which has seen its share of excitement. Now it is enjoying renovated and new housing bringing more people back into the city centre, and the public houses offer a Continental appeal with tables and sunshades for sitting outside. One of the pubs is named 'The Last Drop', appropriately standing not far from the spot where many did make the last drop, for until 1785 the Grassmarket, among its many contributions, provided a public execution place. The executioner was kept particularly busy in Covenanting times when those who were prepared to die for their Presbyterian faith were taken to the scaffold. The site of the gibbet, not far from the city well at the foot of the West Bow, is now marked by a cross set in cobbles and incorporated into the Covenanters' Memorial, with a list of some of those who died there. They included leaders like Sir Archibald Johnston, Lord Warriston, and two young women, Isabel Alison and Marion Harvey, whose crime was to listen to a minister preach. During the Covenanting persecutions 'The human shambles in this place of wailing witnessed executions of this kind almost daily till the 17th of February 1688' when James Renwick, a celebrated field preacher and the last martyr of the Covenant, was executed at the age of 26. More than 100 Covenanters met their end here, and one of the most bitter remarks was made by the Duke of Rothes to a stubborn prisoner: 'Then let him glorify God in the Grassmarket'.

A weekly market was held here from 1477, and in the sixteenth century the corn market was moved to the east end of the square where it operated until last century before moving into a new building on the south side, finally being sited in the then city outskirts at Gorgie. It was not until the mid-seventeenth century that the Grassmarket became the site for executions, the Castle Hill and Mercat Cross being the most common until that time. It is ironic that a city hangman, Alexander Cockburn, met his end in the reign of Charles II on the scaffold where he had meted out similar punishment so often to others. Perhaps the most famous execution – or rather lynching – was perpetrated by the mob itself in 1736. Two smugglers, Andrew Wilson and George Robertson, were sentenced to death for attacking the collector of customs at Pittenweem in Fife, as a revenge for seizures and fines imposed for smuggling offences. Smuggling was generally supported by the Scottish people in

The Grassmarket protest against the revenue men who were often English – or Scotsmen 'chosen on account of their treachery to Scottish interests'.

Lying in the Tolbooth in Edinburgh awaiting their fate, Wilson and Robertson were thwarted in an escape attempt when Wilson, a bulky man, got stuck between the sawn-off bars covering a window. But Wilson felt he had spoiled young Robertson's chances and on the Sunday before execution day when the condemned men were

The foot of the Bow. The West Bow originally zig-zagged from the Lawnmarket into the Grassmarket but was pierced by Victoria Street and Terrace during 19th century 'improvement' schemes. It was down the Bow that the mob stormed to take the unfortunate Captain Porteous to his death.

Victoria Street with its terrace running above the shops is now an 'in' street. With a mixture of restaurants, bars, and a good range of specialist shops it has a charm of its own, but even so there's still a longing for the old closes it replaced.

taken to morning service at St Giles under custody of four soldiers from the City Guard he seized three of them and urged Robertson: 'Run, Geordie, run.' Robertson knocked the fourth guard to the ground and fled, unimpeded by any of the spectators who quickly spread the story round the town where Wilson's plight drew much sympathy. There was talk of a move to rescue him at the Grassmarket, but came the day, April 14, 1736, and the magistrates ensured that a strong detachment of

The Grassmarket the City Guard were on duty. A silent crowd watched the execution, but as it was completed they roared in protest and started hurling whatever was to hand at the Guard. Wilson's body was cut down and an attempt made to carry it off.

The magistrates took refuge in a nearby house, while the City Guard, under their experienced commander Captain John Porteous, tried to make an orderly retreat up the West Bow, still under a hail of missiles.

The West Bow well built in 1674 still stands at the foot of the Bow. On the left are some of the old houses which escaped destruction, including Crockett's Land, built about 1705, and recently restored. On the bend is the foot of Victoria Street. Beyond it is the steeple of the old Highland Tolbooth Church at the head of the Lawnmarket.

His men were being injured, their drum was broken, his pride was hurt, and *The Grassmarket*
Porteous, already in a vile mood because he regarded Robertson's escape as a reflection on his guard, ordered his men 'to level their pieces and be damned'. He snatched a musket from one of the soldiers, and shot dead one of the mob's ringleaders, Charles Husband, who had cut Wilson down. A ragged volley followed and six or seven others fell dead or wounded. The mob were even more incensed and again the Guard were ordered to face them as more stones were hurled. In the narrow press of the West Bow the results were devastating with even people leaning out of their windows being injured and others killed.

Porteous was brought to trial and denied he had ordered his men to fire, but he was sentenced to death. Queen Caroline, who was acting as regent in the absence on

The Covenanters' Memorial in the centre of the Grassmarket marks the spot where men and women died for their faith, 'glorifying God in the Grassmarket'. More than 100 Covenanters were executed here, and the Grassmarket was also a place of public execution, with crowds packing in to see the last throes of criminals.

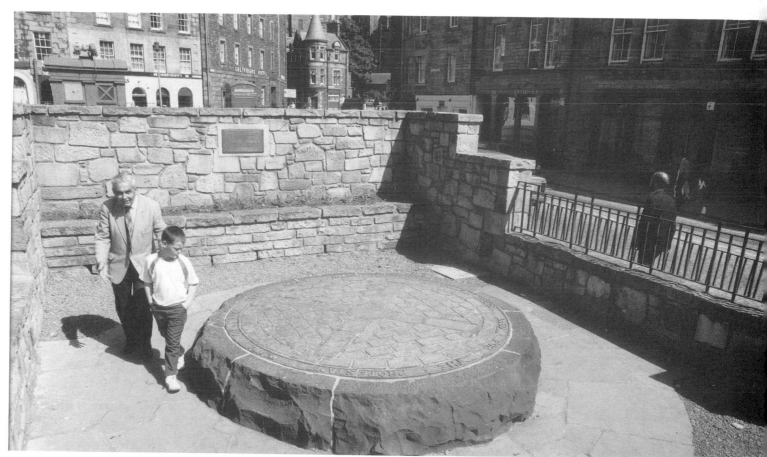

the Continent of George II, ordered the Home Office to give a six weeks' reprieve before granting a full pardon. This was seen in Edinburgh as a gross interference by 'an English government' – it was 40 years after the still-hated Union of Parliaments – and plans were immediately set afoot.

On the night of September 7, the day before that set as Porteous' trial for his execution, a group gathered in the suburb of Portsburgh to the west of the Grassmarket. To the drum beat the mob swelled and then secured various city gates to ensure that troops stationed in the Canongate could not be summoned. Then the City Guardsmen were attacked and disarmed in their guardhouse in the High Street, their muskets, bayonets and Lochaber axes being distributed among the rioters.

On then to the Tolbooth to beat at its outer gates with sledgehammers, bars and axes without success. The mob stacked tar barrels up against the gate and set fire to them, and the gate was breached. They charged through, took the keys from a terrified warder but at first they could find no trace of their target. Porteous, hearing the tumult, had hidden up a chimney, and he had to be hauled down.

They took the now twice condemned man to the Grassmarket, pausing on the way to break into a shop in the Bow and leave a guinea for the length of rope they needed. At the execution place they used a dyer's pole as a gibbet, and the crowd cheered and jeered as the unfortunate Captain was strung up. Shortly afterwards, their work done, the mob dispersed quietly into the night and 'when the morning of the 8th September stole in nothing remained of the event but the fire-blackened cinders of the Tolbooth door, the muskets and Lochaber axes scattered in the streets, and the dead body of Porteous swinging in the breeze. . .' His body was quickly buried in Greyfriars churchyard.

The government was incensed when news reached London, and the Lord Provost of Edinburgh was arrested and held in prison for three weeks; a fine of £2000 was later imposed on the city to go to Porteous' widow. Tempting rewards were offered to identify the ringleaders of the mob that night – some were said to have been dressed as women – but no one came forward.

Nowadays a throng in the Grassmarket turns out for the Saturday fair at Festival time, or is attracted by jazz musicians or other participants in parades starting off or ending in the square. But while the street entertainers might be able to hold a crowd, it is doubtful if anyone now could emulate the feat of an acrobatic Italian father and son who displayed their amazing skill in 1733. They fixed a rope between the Half Moon Battery at the Castle and a point on the south side of the Grassmarket 200 feet below. The father slid down in half a minute while his son repeated the trip blowing a trumpet all the way to the amazement of the huge crowd of spectators.

The Grassmarket is another area where inevitably there have been many changes. The whole of the south side was pulled down and rebuilt at intervals before the end of last century and there has been considerable rebuilding since. The Temple tenements and the Greyfriars monastery were on this side too, the monastery standing opposite where the 1674 Bow Foot well now is. The monasteries of both the Black and Grey Friars were plundered in 1559 at the time of the Reformation and the stones from the two desecrated buildings were put to other uses.

Among the attractions in the Grassmarket was the cockfighting pit at which Deacon Brodie was a frequent gambler, and always well patronised were the inns and hostelries where those attending the markets could eat and sleep or slake a thirst with a customer or crony – 'An pedlars frae the south an' north/Shewed a' their weel stowed boxes forth'. The White Hart Inn, which is still in business, was where the Highland drovers might have sampled the fare, and inevitably Robert Burns stayed there during his last visit to Edinburgh in 1791. The English poet William Wordsworth and his sister opted for the inn also in 1803.

The inns, of course, offered a good view of any trouble in the Grassmarket, and upper rooms were grand circle seats at an execution especially. The annual All Hallow Fair brought the horse and cattle dealers, jugglers and acrobats and all the associated stalls, and the Grassmarket was also a perpetual bustle with carriers bringing in goods from the country. By 1810, 96 carriers arrived weekly.

At the Cowgatehead end stood the King's Head Inn, or Palfrey's, described as one of the best frequented inns in Old Edinburgh. The West Bow which in its time was one of the city's finest streets – 'Up the West Bow for centuries did all that was regal, noble and diplomatic advance on entering the city; and down it, for 124 years between the Restoration and 1784 went more criminals than can be reckoned to their doom, and many a victim of misrule' – plunged very steeply and in a zig-zag from the head of the Lawnmarket into the Grassmarket. It was 'improved' in 1829 by hauling down its middle section. The lower part was left with some splendid late seventeenth- and early eighteenth-century houses as Victoria Street with its terraces was created as part of the general scheme introduced under the 1827 Improvement Act which also fixed the line of the Mound to the High Street. Victoria Street is now a handsome curve with shops, restaurants and bars, a very 'in' thoroughfare where on occasion traders have even hired their own town crier to warn shoppers when the traffic wardens are about to descend!

Among the evocatively named buildings to vanish were Clockmaker's Land, which took its name from an eminent watchmaker, and Mahogany Land which had an outer stair protected by a screen of wood. The old Bowhead (pages 22 and 136)suffered a similar fate in a frenzy of Victorian redevelopment. Other streets angle off the Grassmarket. To the north-west runs King's Stables Road, called after the royal mews used when jousting tournaments were held on the low ground beneath the castle rock in the time of King James IV. There is a record too of knights in the sixteenth century challenging to mortal combat 'upon the Baresse the place accustomed and of old appointed for triell of such matters'.

At the end of the road stands St Cuthbert's Church, which was probably originally founded by Malcolm Canmore and his Queen, Margaret. It is certainly mentioned in a charter granted by their son David I in or about 1127. The present church was built in 1892-95, although the 1789 steeple was retained. The churchyard also has a watch tower to guard against the Resurrectionists who in the early years of the nineteenth century particularly dug up the graves of newly buried bodies and secretly conveyed the corpses to anatomists anxious for dissection material to show their students. One of the best-known anatomists in the city was Dr Robert Knox, and his enthusiasm to have 'fresh' material to work on closed his eyes to its source, but it was to give Edinburgh two of its most infamous rogues. Their reputation endures to this day.

We return to the Grassmarket, and take the other westerly road, up the West Port where the ancient burghs of Eastern and Western Portsburgh once held sway until they were incorporated in Edinburgh in 1648. The West Port is another part of the Old Town undergoing a housing transformation – new and renovated buildings line the still narrow street which originally provided one of the main entrances into the town.

But in 1827 the cramped and dirty closes housed a rougher element, including many of the Irish workers and their families who found employment digging out the Union Canal from Edinburgh to Falkirk. Among them were William Burke and William Hare, and their activities were to earn them literally worldwide notoriety and an everlasting place in the city's story.

From 1505 the town council had allowed the Incorporation of Surgeons and Barbers to have annually the body of a condemned man for anatomical purposes, and this was later stepped up to include bodies of people who died in the correction house. But by the eighteenth century, as medicine advanced and the need to experiment and teach expanded, bodies were shipped to Edinburgh surgeons from London, and Edinburgh folk arranged for railings or a heavy mort stone to be placed over a fresh grave to deter grave robbers. The anatomy classes were full, and by 1827 no fewer than six anatomy lecturers were teaching in the Surgeons' Square area. In November of that year two men were directed by a student to Dr Knox's rooms at 10 Surgeons' Square where they offered a body which the good doctor bought for £7 10s. The vendors were Burke, who was born in County Tyrone and came to Scotland in 1818, and his fellow-Irishman Hare, generally regarded as the more devious of the two. Burke had fallen in with Helen Dougal or McDougal and they eventually lived as man and wife, moving into Edinburgh and staying in the Beggars' Hotel, a lodging house, in Portsburgh. There they met Hare and his wife. He had also come from Ireland to work on the canal and lived in a tramps' lodging house in Tanner's Close in the West

There's plenty of fun in the Grassmarket, and this is where the Jazz Festival parade ends up during the Edinburgh Festival. It's time for an impromptu solo, with plenty of encouragement from the flapper girls.

Port. Mrs Hare was the widow of his former landlord in the house. When in 1827 an old army pensioner died in the lodging house, Hare said he was owed £4 by the man, and he thought he could sell the body to square things. His lodger Burke, who had by then moved into the close, was enlisted in the ploy and they took the body to Knox whose assistants told the pair they would be glad to see them again when they had another body to dispose of.

The Irishmen saw their chance to make money and so started on a trail of at least 16 murders to provide the bodies – they were not Resurrectionists in that there is no proof they opened graves: they found their victims by other means. Throughout 1828 they suffocated people lured usually to Hare's lodging house – a miller, an Englishman, an old beggarwoman, an elderly woman and her dumb grandson – people who would not be particularly missed. But among their victims was a young girl Mary Paterson, who had friends in the city, and their last two murders, both committed in October, were to be their ultimate downfall.

James Wilson was a simple laddie, Daft Jamie to all who knew him, and physically big and strong for his 18 years. Burke decoyed him to Hare's house and plied him with drink before they had a struggle to strangle him. Three days later Burke noticed an Irish beggarwoman Mary Docherty, and invited her to the house where she was offered a bed. After a late-night drinking party she was strangled. Another lodger in the morning lifted a bundle of straw and found the woman's naked body. The police were told and Burke and Mrs McDougal were taken into custody. Later the Hares were also arrested, but all denied any involvement in Mrs Docherty's death and indeed said they had never seen her before, either alive or dead.

Sixteen murders were admitted by Burke in a confession after the trial, but for the Crown the problem was one of proof of any killings. Eventually the Lord Advocate, the leading Scottish prosecutor, decided to indict Burke and McDougal for the murders of Mary Paterson, Daft Jamie and Mrs Docherty, and agreement was made with Hare to turn King's evidence. The trial was set for Christmas Eve and the prisoners were brought from the Calton Jail to the cells below the Justiciary Court House in Parliament Close. Such was the interest in the case that crowds were waiting to hear it, 'and by nine o'clock, when the doors were opened, every available inch of space was crowded to suffocation'.

Among the advocates before the bench of four judges was Henry Cockburn (later Lord Cockburn) who represented McDougal, and other eminent counsel were in both the defence and prosecution line-up. After legal argument, the Lord Advocate Sir William Rae agreed to proceed with the murder of Mrs Docherty first. The prisoners pleaded not guilty, and the jury was empanelled.

In those days a trial went on until it was over, and the prosecution case was outlined first of all by several witnesses. But the highlight for the packed court room was the

Another view of the Castle from the west end of the Grassmarket. King's Stables Road leads to another old church, St Cuthbert's. It was in the closes off the West Port at this end of the Grassmarket that Burke and Hare engaged in murder to procure the bodies to keep Dr Knox going in his anatomy classes.

appearance on the witness stand of William Hare – 'that miscreant entered with a ghastly smile and gave his infamous testimony with unblushing effrontery. He saw his neck was safe,' said one commentator. Hare said Burke had killed Mrs Docherty, and in cross-examination declined to answer many of Cockburn's questions.

No witnessess were called for the defence, and the Lord Advocate addressed the jury. It was three in the morning when Burke's counsel rose to speak (now 17 hours into the trial) and Henry Cockburn began his address at 5am. An hour later the

115

Lord Justice-Clerk charged the jury and at 8.30 on Christmas morning they retired to consider their verdict. Fifty minutes later they reappeared to say they found Burke guilty of Mrs Docherty's murder, and the charge against McDougal not proven. 'Nelly, you are out of the scrape,' Burke said. Lord Justice-Clerk Boyle pronounced the death sentence – by hanging on January 28, with Burke's body being publicly dissected and anatomised. 'And I trust that if it is ever customary to preserve skeletons yours will be preserved, in order that posterity may keep in remembrance your atrocious crime,' added the judge.

Edinburgh rejoiced in Burke's sentence but there were misgivings about McDougal's acquittal. The deaths of Mary Paterson and Daft Jamie were still unexplained and unavenged. When she was released Helen McDougal narrowly escaped lynching and had to be rescued by the police. Even in Newcastle to where she fled she was recognised and attacked. Eventually she is said to have died in Australia in 1868.

Mrs Hare was released from prison about three weeks after the trial when it was accepted that her husband would not be prosecuted, and she also had to be rescued from the mob before leaving the city and eventually heading back to Ireland.

Burke in the meantime had made a very full confession to the Edinburgh *Courant* and an 'official' confession before the Sheriff, both of which were published after his death. The morning of Wednesday, January 28, brought torrential rain but people were not going to miss the 'great event', as it was described.

> 'By 8am the largest crowd of spectators – estimated at between 20,000 and 25,000 – ever collected in the streets of Edinburgh thronged the spacious area of the Lawnmarket and its approaches. Each window in the towering lands, which reared their then unbroken frames on either side of the historic plaza, had been long before "bespoke" at prices ranging from 5s to 20s, according to the facilities afforded for viewing the last agonies of the criminal. All fashionable Edinburgh had a seat.'

The mob cried for Hare while Burke's body dangled for an hour before it was cut down. Early the next day it was taken to the Surgeons' College for public dissection by Professor Alexander Monro, who then lectured on the murderer's brain. But a riot broke out as students protested they could not get in to see the body.

On the Friday arrangements were made for what was described as a 'grand public exhibition'. Burke was laid out on a black marble slab in the anatomical theatre and a total of 30,000 are reckoned to have passed through the room to see the corpse, doubtless many of them reviling it. Burke's body was subsequently further dissected and pieces used in further lectures. His skeleton, as His Lordship wished, was displayed in the Anatomical Museum of the University of Edinburgh, and can still be seen today.

What of the others? Hare, finally immune from prosecution, had eventually to be smuggled out of jail and into a mail coach for Dumfries. News of his arrival spread like wildfire and a crowd of 8000 gathered to see the villain. He had to be rescued by the police and spent the night in the town jail for his own protection before being told to move on. He was last positively seen on the road near Carlisle, although there is a tale that he was later recognised by fellow-workmen who threw him into a lime pit, causing the loss of his sight. A blind beggar on the streets of London in the '50s and '60s was said to be Hare.

Dr Knox, who had been an immensely popular and successful lecturer with more than 500 students in his classes at the time of the trial, was roundly attacked in the Press. A mob burned his effigy outside his house. He continued to lecture, however, although the number of his students gradually dropped. He tried unsuccessfully for professorial chairs but no university would have him.

Knox then moved to London where he lectured and wrote, and latterly had a practice in Hackney where he died of apoplexy in 1862 at the age of 71. He lives on in James Bridie's play, *The Anatomist*.

CHAPTER 9 GREYFRIARS

THE OTHER main street running off the Grassmarket is Candlemaker Row, a steep brae named very logically after those who worked there. By the beginning of the sixteenth century candle-making had become a specialised industry in the town. The Candlemakers' Incorporation was formed before 1517 and was highly prosperous until gas lighting came along early last century.

The candlemakers, however, were regarded as a nuisance because of the smell of their melting tallow and the danger of fires, and the town council decreed they could not have their workshops on main thoroughfares. In 1654, after a workshop in Forrester's Wynd off the Cowgate caught fire, the council decided that the candlemakers must be properly segregated, and the Incorporation was granted the use of waste ground near the Society Port in the Flodden Wall to the east of Greyfriars churchyard. In 1722 they built their convening hall in a tenement at No 36 Candlemaker Row, and the date is still visible although the coat of arms and motto have been worn away. Today a candle shop still exists in the street, at the top of which is one of the most familiar statues in Edinburgh, the life-size Greyfriars Bobby which sits atop a now disused fountain.

The dog is buried inside the Greyfriars kirkyard opposite, a tribute to the faithfulness of the Skye terrier which guarded his master's grave for many years and won a special place in the townsfolk's affection. The dog died on January 14, 1872, but not before becoming something of a legend.

Bobby was the household pet of Constable John Gray and his family who lived in a one-room house in Hall's Court in the Cowgate. 'Auld Jock' had trained Bobby to grip the legs of anyone who attacked him while on patrol, and so he was both pet and bodyguard, and an animal well known in the area.

Gray's hazardous work in all weathers took its toll and he died from tuberculosis in 1858, being buried in Greyfriars churchyard. Bobby was at the funeral and afterwards was taken home. He was soon scratching at the door to get out, and ran up Candlemaker Row to get back to the graveside of his master. The gardener found him there in the morning and fed him. Every day and night thereafter Bobby was to be found 'on guard'. Passing policemen gave him titbits, and he found light entertainment in chasing away the cats which prowled round the gravestones. No matter how often he was tempted by food or other diversions, however, Bobby always returned to the grave to resume his vigil.

A restaurant proprietor, John Traill, took over giving the dog his meals, and he went to court on Bobby's behalf when the town council ordered all dogs to be licensed or destroyed. Eventually Lord Provost William Chambers agreed to pay the licence himself and had a collar made and inscribed 'Greyfriars Bobby from the Lord

An Edinburgh worthy relaxes for a moment beside Greyfriars Bobby's statue, while tourists get the spiel as they pass the memorial to the trusty little dog which, like his master, is buried in Greyfriars Kirkyard across the street. When he died in 1872 Bobby had become a legend in the city, with the Lord Provost paying for his collar. Walt Disney made a film about Greyfriars Bobby.

Greyfriars Kirk, or correctly the Greyfriars Tolbooth and Highland Kirk following a series of congregational amalgamations. It was built in the gardens of the monastery of the Grey Friars, the order founded by St Francis of Assisi. At Greyfriars the National Covenant was signed publicly in 1683.

Provost, 1867, licensed'. The court case brought fame and he was for ever painted and sketched. As old age came and his bones could not stand a dreich Edinburgh winter, he was taken into Traill's home, and when he died he was secretly buried by Traill and a few friends in Greyfriars, their task done stealthily because burial of animals there was forbidden.

An Englishwoman, Baroness Angela Burdett-Coutts, who had heard the story, offered to donate a suitable memorial, and the fountain was unveiled on November 15, 1873. For her generosity she was given the freedom of the city. Now a stone erected by the Dog Aid Society recalls Bobby's devotion, and Auld Jock's grave is also well marked with a fresh stone erected by Americans who were enthralled by the story of Greyfriars Bobby, which was made into a Disney film. Greyfriars Kirk itself, or to give it its modern title following the amalgamation of various congregations – Greyfriars Tolbooth and Highland Kirk – was built on the garden of the monastery of the Grey Friars which, as we have seen, stood on the south side of the Grassmarket at the foot of Candlemaker Row. The order, founded by St Francis of Assisi, seems to have appeared in Scotland for the first time around 1231. After the Reformation and the destruction of their monastery the friars fled to the Netherlands and the town council cast their eyes on the now vacant site, desperate as they were for a new burying ground. The one beside St Giles was already overcrowded, and they obtained Royal sanction in 1562.

By the end of the sixteenth century the council also decided there was a need for more churches as the then four parishes were meeting in St Giles. In 1602 they set aside £500 to build a new church at Greyfriars, which was finally opened in 1620 – the first Reformed kirk to be built in the city. Tradition has it that the National Covenant was signed on February 28, 1638, on a tombstone in the yard, but it was almost certainly within the church itself. Some Covenanters were said to have signed with their own blood to show the depth of their feelings. In the 'killing times' which followed the Restoration of Charles II and his determination to enforce the Episcopal form of worship on the country, Covenanting prisoners taken at the Battle of Bothwell Bridge in 1679 were brought to Edinburgh and more than 1000 were crushed into the ground beside the southern section of the churchyard for more than five months. (The narrow south burial yard now called the 'Covenanters' Prison' was not enclosed and added to the kirkyard until 1703.) Men and women were exposed to all weather and the daily food provided by the Episcopal-dominated Privy Council was 'one penny loaf to each prisoner'. Some died from cold and hunger, others were put to torture before joining the martyrs in the Grassmarket. Between 200 and 300 of the Covenanters who refused to sign a bond not to take up arms against the king were marched to Leith and put aboard a ship for transportation to the colonies as slaves. The vessel was driven onto the rocks at Orkney in a severe storm and more than 200 of the prisoners drowned. The kirk also served as a barracks for Cromwell's troops between 1650 and 1653 and as a gunpowder store, which resulted in an explosion in 1718 causing considerable damage to the west end of the building, by then serving two congregations.

A new church was then built at the west end similar to the truncated old one (the cost was met from a duty on ale), and for many years Greyfriars and New Greyfriars worshipped side by side. In 1938 the 1718 dividing wall was removed and the building opened up into one church. It contains many interesting exhibits, including an original copy of the National Covenant. Because the old Highland church is now incorporated, there is a service in Gaelic on Sunday afternoons. The kirkyard itself contains the bodies of many famous Scots, the first notable to be interred being

The impressive driveway leading to George Heriot's School, one of the original hospitals donated by
wealthy Edinburgh merchants for the poor children of the town. Heriot's is now one of the largest
co-educational fee-paying schools in Edinburgh, a fitting tribute to its founder, 'Jinglin' Geordie.'

James Douglas, Earl of Morton, the regent executed in 1581. The architect of the
first stage of the New Town, James Craig, who died in 1795, lies there, as do
wealthy merchants whose benefactions gave Edinburgh famous hospital schools,
John Watson and George Watson. Here too is Captain John Porteous, a modern
stone marking the spot, while a huge circular mausoleum is a tribute to Sir George
Mackenzie of Rosehaugh, author of many legal works and the man largely respon-
sible for the foundation of the Advocates' – now the National – Library on George
IV Bridge. But as King's Advocate he earned the epithet 'Bluidy Mackenzie' from
the Covenanters whose own Martyrs' Monument is an impressive piece of statuary.

The Kirkyard of Greyfriars contains many fascinating tombstones and is probably the richest of all the
Old Town graveyards in this respect. Behind the wall is Merchant Street, with the Public Library in the
background on George IV Bridge.

Indeed of all the old city graveyards, Greyfriars is probably the richest in monuments; it also offers some splendid views of the city, and under its shady trees is the perfect place to pause to reflect on the often tempestuous lives of the characters who are at last at peace here.

Walk through the churchyard past the line of the old Flodden Wall and west yard and you enter the grounds of one of the city's most renowned schools, George Heriot's, whose foundation was a rich man's gift to the city he loved. The Heriot family originally came from East Lothian but George Heriot's grandfather moved into the town. His son, also George, a goldsmith, became an important man, representing the city in Parliament and being appointed to the deputation sent to plead with King James VI when he threatened to transfer his court to Linlithgow after riots in 1596.

The young George Heriot was born in 1563 and served an apprenticeship with his father. As a young man he set up his own booth near St Giles and built up an extensive trade as a goldsmith and banker. Such was his expertise and reputation that he was proclaimed at the Cross goldsmith to Anne of Denmark, the queen of James VI. He was then 34, and four years later in 1601 he was appointed jeweller to the king himself. James frequently borrowed from Heriot and in 1603, at the Union of the Crowns, the monarch was supplied by him with an abundant collection of rings to distribute among the English nobility on his triumphant journey south. Heriot took up house in London and his advice and assistance were eagerly sought at court. Canny Scot, though, he remained – as security for loans he held in a strong room jewellery and plate belonging to James and Anne, and for a time even the title deeds of the Chapel Royal at Stirling.

By 1620 he had amassed a fortune and the nickname 'Jinglin' Geordie' to go with it. He had land outside the city, and he also started to make provision for his long-cherished project 'to found and erect ane publick pious and charitable work' similar to Christ's Hospital in London. Heriot died in 1624 in London, and although his father was buried in Greyfriars almost in shadow of the school, its founder was interred in St Martin-in-the-Fields.

Under the terms of the deeds by which the hospital, or Heriot's Wark, was formed, Heriot left the bulk of his estate to maintain and educate the destitute sons of burgesses and freemen of the burgh. The foundation stone of the north-west tower was laid on July 1, 1628 on land bought from the council and then bounded by the Flodden Wall and the Telfer Wall to the south. Building was slow and it was not until 1659 that the first foundationers moved into what has been described as 'a prodigy of Scots Renaissance architecture'. The boys, from seven to 17, had to wear cloth doublet, breeks and stockings of 'sad russet' in colour, with black hats. The hospital school was run very much unaltered with both boarders and day pupils until 1885 when there was a change in the schooling system to make Heriot's a secondary day *Greyfriars* school open to fee-paying scholars. The school's first session under the new regime began in September 1886 with about 400 pupils. Like most of the other big fee-paying schools in Edinburgh, many founded originally as hospitals after Heriot's example by men like George and John Watson, Daniel Stewart, William Fettes and James Gillespie, Heriot's has gone co-educational.

The Vennel runs from Lauriston Place to the Grassmarket, a narrow pedestrian lane which passes Heriot's School. An original tower from the Flodden Wall can still be seen at the top of the Vennel steps.

Just to the west of the school grounds is the Vennel, which lay immediately outside both the Telfer and Flodden Walls. An original tower in the Flodden Wall can still be seen at the head of the Vennel which runs from the West Port to Lauriston Place.

The land which lay just outside the Telfer Wall of 1628-36 was the new site for the Royal Infirmary which had its origins firmly inside the Old Town, and whose inspiration came from the physicians and surgeons already working there. One of the leading surgeons was John Monro who published a pamphlet in 1721 to arouse interest in the building of a public hospital, an appeal which had no success at the time. Four years later a second and successful attempt was made, backed by Lord Provost George Drummond and by the Royal College of Physicians.

A meeting of subscribers was held in February 1728, and later that month the first minute of the Royal Infirmary confirmed the capital sum of £2000 for the building was guaranteed. The first infirmary was opened in 1729 in a building in Robertson's Close, one of the steep alleys still rising south from the Cowgate. The first patient, Elizabeth Sinclair, a native of Caithness, was admitted to one of the six beds, suffering from anaemia. The 'little house', as it was called, prospered, and the infirmary's capital fund also increased so that in 1736 the board of management felt they should buy the nearby Thomson's Yard for a new building, ground which had originally belonged to the Black Friars who had themselves built a small infirmary. The new hospital's foundation stone was laid in 1738 and the patients transferred from Robertson's Close in 1741, although it was a further seven years before building work was completed.

Ultimately the new infirmary too needed to be expanded to keep pace with the demands put on it, and there were protests that the site in Infirmary Street was becoming hemmed in. There was talk of expansion on the existing site or transferring to the open ground owned and occupied by George Watson's Hospital at Lauriston and above the Meadows (formerly the old Burgh Loch which was drained in 1740). The latter was finally chosen, not without some opposition from some owners with interests in the land – Watson's had to move to the old Merchant Maiden Hospital at the foot of Archibald Place – and in October 1870 the Prince of Wales with appropriate ceremony laid the foundation stone of the new Royal Infirmary which today is recognised as one of the finest teaching hospitals in the world.

Following the line of Telfer's Wall eastwards along Lauriston Place and into Forrest Road brings us back to the top of Candlemaker Row where the Bristo (or Society or Grey Friars) Port stood. Close by were buildings called Society which formed a quadrangle with open, tree-planted ground sloping down to the Cowgate. They were built by a society of brewers formed in 1598 and the ground formerly belonged to the convent of Sienna (at Sciennes across the Burgh Loch).

An Englishman who visited the town in 1598 observed, 'the better type of citi-

In so many parts of the Old Town there is the unexpected. This little group of buildings in Brown's Place nestles on the Vennel steps above the Grassmarket, while over all the familiar outline of the castle dominates the scene.

zens brew ale, their usual drink, which will distemper a stranger's body'. The usual allowance at table at that time was a chopin, equal to about an imperial pint, for each person.

With so much brewing around and small brewers selling their produce in many of the closes, drunkenness was a common sight. In the Canongate it was resolved to restrict the sale of ale on the Sabbath at least and the bailies there forbade that drinks be available 'doune to the tyme of preaching'. It was with the aim of establishing a public company to manufacture beer on a large scale that the town council suggested the formation of 'The Fellowship and Society of Ale and Beer Brewers of the Burgh of Edinburgh'. The vats and brewing houses were set up on the land at the Bristo Port, water would be pumped by windmill from the Burgh Loch, and as a final encouragement only the Society would be allowed to 'furnish good and sufficient ale to all burghers'.

However, there were rows over the land and over the use of the Burgh Loch, while the quality of the beer was causing dissatisfaction. According to the city fathers: 'The Society daily contravened the Acts by selling the ale above twelve pennies the pint . . . Besides their ale and small drink was not of sufficient strength relative to the price'. By Act of Council the Society was dissolved in 1618 but the name attached itself to the area, and the last of Society was finally demolished in the 1870s to make way for Chambers Street.

Outside the Bristo Port stood three buildings only too well known to the townsfolk, the charity workhouse, the correction house, and Bedlam, the asylum. The bedlam site lay between what is now Forrest Road and Bristo Place, and it was here that the poet Fergusson died in 1774 at the age of 24 after injuries received in a fall unbalanced his mind.

THE UNIVERSITY

*E*DINBURGH NOW has two universities which attract students and postgraduates from many parts of the world. The Heriot-Watt University whose campus has moved to Riccarton on the western side of the city reached full status from the old Heriot-Watt College based in Chambers Street and the Grassmarket. In 1989 the doors finally closed on the Chambers Street building, which will be converted into a new court-house.

But Edinburgh University is firmly rooted inside the town, with its origins at Kirk o' Field where Darnley was blown to an untimely death by his enemies. It is the youngest of the old Scottish universities, after St Andrews, Glasgow and Aberdeen. In 1558 Robert Reid, Bishop of Orkney, bequeathed to Edinburgh 8000 merks to build a university, and in 1581 the town council began to form a college, blessed with a charter from King James VI, in the following year. On the site of Kirk o' Field, 'a quaint group of quadrangular buildings' grew up gradually to form the college – 'Three courts, the southern of which was occupied on two sides by the classrooms and professors' houses and on the others by the College Hall, the houses of the principal and the resident graduates'.

In 1583 the council brought Robert Rollock, a professor at St Andrews, to be a professor at Edinburgh and his reputation brought the first students to the new university. 'It was the fashion of the time.' writes Arnot, 'not that the masters in the university should adhere each to a particular profession, but that the same professor who began giving lectures on humanity [Latin] to his students should proceed with them in the branches of mathematics and philosophy, till their course was finished, and the students had received the degree of Master of Arts'.

But in Edinburgh it seemed the first students were lacking in their knowledge of Latin, essential for their studies (lectures were given in Latin), and a second professor, Duncan Nairn, was appointed to make good this failing. Rollock became principal of the college although he continued to teach his class and later became professor of divinity, combining his various roles successfully until 1620. As principal he was also expected to preach weekly in St Giles.

It was tough going for the early students; the session started at the beginning of October and lasted till the end of the following August when an examination took place before the town council who were the college patrons and senior members of

The dramatic entrance to the Old College of Edinburgh University on South Bridge. 'Nothing in Scotland is grander' than the frontage designed by Robert Adam whose original concept for the inner building was developed by William Playfair. The dome was added in 1879, with the figure of Youth bearing aloft the torch of learning.

the university.

The name of Lord Provost George Drummond is linked almost inevitably with the development of the university – we have seen how he gave the Royal Infirmary a vital push and how his vision opened up the way for the New Town. He wanted to enhance the university's reputation for the benefit of the city. He urged the council to give practical support for expansion and to attract students from overseas. He also persuaded the council in 1726, during the first of his six terms as Lord Provost, to accept that it would be 'of great advantage to this college, city and country that medicine in all its branches be professed here by such a number of professors of that science as may by themselves promote students'.

In 1720 Alexander Monro had been appointed Professor of Anatomy at the university, and between them Drummond and Monro were to ensure the eventual formation of a medical school which, along with the Royal Infirmary, took Edinburgh into the front rank of medicine, attracting some of the greatest men of the day to teach, while their qualified students then went out to spread their own learning. Monro himself was succeeded by his son who in turn was followed by his own son in the Anatomy chair, a family influence extending over 120 years in all.

While they still had time for the odd diversions, such as the occasional riot, many of the students worked long and hard, and came from poor backgrounds. There is a record in 1826, for instance, of the student who 'breakfasted on porridge and milk, and had for dinner, three days a week, broth and a little meat; on the other days bread and milk, sometimes potatoes and herrings; he had tea in the afternoon but no supper'. The same report noted there were also students 'who scarcely ever allowed themselves candles, and wrote their exercises, and prepared their lessons, by the light of the fire. Many others do not use fire, except in the evening, and some not even then'.

There had been increasing pressure to replace the buildings in which the university began with something more in keeping with its burgeoning reputation. An Italian visitor in 1788 wrote: 'What is called a college is nothing more than a mass of ruined buildings of very ancient construction'. In 1785 Henry Dundas (later Viscount Melville) revived the idea of a new building, and soon afterwards the magistrates and council launched an appeal for funds for this purpose. At this time the South Bridge was being built over the Cowgate to open up the South Side, and feus along the bridge were to go towards the cost of the new university building, to be designed by the architect Robert Adam. He had prepared two plans for a southern approach to the city, both including preliminary designs for a new university. In one a semicircular crescent was laid out in front of the university.

James Craig, whose plan for the New Town was accepted after open competition, also prepared a 'Plan for Improving the City of Edinburgh' in 1786 in which he proposed a more grandiose concept than the council would accept. He wanted a large octagonal space round the Tron Kirk and he too envisaged a crescent, south-facing, and extending 500 feet from the west end of the university area. Had either Adam's or Craig's dreams reflecting the spaciousness of the New Town been accepted for the southern approaches, then an excitingly different prospect to the narrow South Bridge would have faced us today.

There seemed unanimous agreement, however, that the university was on the correct site, close to the Royal Infirmary. In 1789 therefore the town council agreed that the Adam plan for the new building should be accepted, and with due ceremony on November 16 of that year the foundation stone was laid by Lord Napier, the Grand Master Mason of Scotland. There was trouble raising the £40,000 required to complete the building which had to be altered from the Adam concept. The building which stands today on the corner of Chambers Street and South Bridge still retains many of his important features, however, including four sides enclosing a court, although he wanted a transverse forecourt leading to a square quadrangle beyond.

In 1792 Adam died, and when the Napoleonic War broke out the following year building operations ground to a halt as money had to be diverted to the war. A bad harvest also meant a population dependent on relief and the subscribers faced great difficulties in raising any money to advance the work. In 1799 the trustees, in a plea for government help, had to report that although some accommodation was available, work had stopped, 'leaving a considerable part of the east and north fronts unroofed, and the beams and joisting exposed to the injury of the weather; the college area at the same time embarrassed with sheds, stones and other materials'.

The 1300 students were suffering 'greater inconveniences than were felt during the miserable state of the old buildings'. A dwarf called Geordie More is even said to have built a wee hut at the college site and lived there unchallenged until the work was finally restarted after Parliament in 1815 granted £10,000 annually for ten years. It was not completed until 1834.

While the outside of the quadrangle is Adam ('his greatest public work'), the inside is by William Playfair. 'Nothing in Scotland is grander than Adam's entrance front,' says one commentator of the magnificence of what we call the Old College, the heart of the university which has expanded dramatically into many buildings across the South Side. Among Playfair's great contributions possibly the gem is the Upper Library, which has been described as 'one of the greatest glories of the university, which is one of the finest achievements of late classical architecture in Britain, and which can stand comparison, although it is in quite a different style, with the justly celebrated Wren Library at Trinity College, Cambridge'.

Lord Provost Drummond died in 1766 at the age of 79, his visions on the way to fulfilment. Another contribution he made to the town has subsequently fallen under the university's mantle. This is St Cecilia's Hall, nestling in the Cowgate at the foot

Inside the old Quad the magnificence of the building is evident. Among Playfair's particular triumphs in the university is the Upper Library, although even his original design has been altered in its construction.

of Niddry Street. Drummond joined the Edinburgh Musical Society in 1752 and in 1756 became its deputy governor. The Society organised musical evenings and in 1759 decided to build 'a new musick room'.

So the hall was constructed, and Lord Cockburn described it as 'the best and most beautiful concert-room I have ever yet seen. And there I have myself seen most of our literary and fashionable gentlemen, predominating with their side curls and frills, and ruffles, and silver buckles; and our stately matrons stiffened in hoops and gorgeous satin; and our beauties with high-heeled shoes, powdered and pomatumed hair, and lofty and composite head-dresses'. The oval concert room, frequently used for recitals and a regular Festival venue, is believed to be based by the architect Robert Mylne on the opera house at Parma in Italy.

When the Society disbanded in 1800 the hall became a Baptist chapel for a while and then served as the Grand Lodge of Scotland from 1809 to 1844. A plain frontage was added and during its life it had had various subsequent uses until it was restored in the 1970s by the University. The Russell Collection of early keyboard instruments is housed there, and is open to the public.

It was appropriate that on the night of December 20, 1766 a 'grand funeral concert' was held there by the Musical Society to mark George Drummond's death. 'The music was solemn and plaintive, finely adapted to the occasion, conducted with dignity, and performed with taste.' One of the many tributes to the man who forged lasting links between Town and Gown and who helped Edinburgh University to attain the outstanding position in the world of learning and research it holds today.

The university accommodation has spread across the city from the Old Quad, unfortunately at one time destroying most of the fine old George Square in a mid-century plan to create a new central campus, but its presence and contribution to city life through its teaching staff and its students is inestimable.

But let the worthy Lord Cockburn, defender of the appearance of the city, have a final say about the University and the Old College in particular: 'When the College was begun, it was in a large piece of nearly open ground; laid out chiefly in gardens. There were no houses on its eastern or southern sides; nothing on its west except rubbish, that could easily have been bought; and nothing on its north side that did much harm. It might have stood, though rimmed by street, with much turfed and shrubberied space beyond this rim; with little noise; and the possibility of being seen.'

'It is now jostled by houses all round; without a foot of soil except what it stand on. To be sure, the spare-ground could not have been kept clear without a price; and, considering how long and ominously the College itself remained unfinished for want of funds, nobody perhaps is blameable for its present state. But it is an example, and a striking one, of danger that might have been avoided, and of the imprudence of letting such things take their own course, and trusting to accidental deliverance. What has happened should either have been foreseen and prevented; or the College ought not to have been placed where it is, and probably would not. As it is, it is nearly lost, externally, as an ornament to the town.'

He might have been right about its immediate surroundings, but he was writing before the great dome was built, in 1879, with the gilded figure of Youth bearing the torch of learning, now an eye-catching feature of the city skyline.

THEN AND NOW

*E*DINBURGH has charmed visitors throughout the years and won glowing acclaim – the most pleasant city in the land in which to live was a recent accolade. But it was not always so, as diarists have recorded. Queen Margaret in 1255 in a list of grievances complained that she was confined to the Castle, 'a sad and solitary place, without verdure, and by reason of its vicinity to the sea, unwholesome'. Her views might have been prejudiced – she was English and very young at the time.

The French historian Froissart, writing about his countrymen in the city in 1384-5 to help King Robert II against the English, described it as 'Paris in Scotland'. He suggests that the townsfolk lived in houses which could quickly be rebuilt if they were destroyed by invaders' fire – perhaps only a few pieces of wood as the main support with a roof of branches.

By the early sixteenth century the building style at least was changed – 'The city is not built of bricks, but of unhewn and square stones, so that few cities can compare with it in large palaces'. Down the High Street, writes Alexander Alesse, a former canon at St Andrews, were

'some fine houses on both sides, and the most of them built of polished stone. There is another street, called the Canongate, which is narrower, and is separated from the High Street by a wall, with a gate and tower, and is considered a suburb.

'From the High Street there extend both to the north and south many alleys; all of which are replenished with lofty houses; as is also the Cowgate, in which dwell the great men and senators of the city, and in which there are palaces belonging to the princes of the kingdom – nothing there being humble or plain, but all magnificent.'

In 1598 Fynes Moryson, 'gentleman', visited Edinburgh and found it

'high seated, in a fruitful soyle and wholesome aire, and is adorned with many noblemen's towers lying about it, and aboundeth with many springs of sweet waters'.

Then and Now

'From the King's Palace (Holyrood) at the east, the city still riseth higher and higher towards the west, and consists especially of one broad and very faire street, (which is the greatest part and sole ornament thereof), the rest of the side streets and allies being of poore building, and inhabited with very poore people, and this length from the east to the west is about a mile, whereas the bredth of the city from the north to the south is narrow, and cannot be halfe a mile. At the furthest end towards the west, is a very strong Castle, which the Scots hold unexpungable.

Edinburgh as it might have been. . . this sketch shows the head of the West Bow in 1843. Johnston Terrace has been carved to run below the castle to join the Lawnmarket and the distinctive Bowhead was replaced in what has been described as one of the worst acts of vandalism in the Old Town.

Very fou

A common enough sight in the last century when cheap drink helped many a man get through the day. This sketch is by Walter Geikie, the deaf and dumb artist, who was born in 1795. His pen vividly captured many scenes of Edinburgh street life.

To the north and south outside the town walls were 'fruitful fields of corn'.

'The houses are built of unpolished stone, and in the faire street good part of them is of free stone, which in that broade streete would make a faire shew, but that the outsides of them are faced with wooden galleries, built upon the second story of the house; yet these galleries give the owners a faire and pleasant prospect, into

137

the said faire and broad streete, when they sit or stand in the same. The walls of the city are built of little and unpolished stones, and seeme ancient, but are very narrow, and in some places exceeding low, in others, ruined.'

Another French visitor, the Duc de Rohan, journeyed to Edinburgh in 1600 and said of the High Street:

'As to the buildings, they are not very sumptuous; for almost all the houses are formed of wood. But to make up for this they are so well filled with inhabitants, that I believe there is no city so populous as this, considering its size. But it would be against all reason if it were otherwise; for, in the first place, it is situated in the more fertile regions of Scotland – as is demonstrated by there being more than a hundred gentlemen's seats within two leagues of the city.'

John Taylor, who won some renown as the Water Poet (he was at one time a waterman in London), found the Royal Mile 'the fairest and goodliest street that ever mine eyes beheld'. And he enjoyed himself too.

'There I found entertainment beyond my expectations and merit; and there is fish, flesh, bread, and fruit, in such variety, that I think I may offenceless call it superfluite and satietie. The worst was, that wine and ale was so scarce and the people then such misers of it, that every night before I went to bed, if any man had asked me a civil question, all the wit in my head could not have made him a sober answer.'

Thus he wrote in his *Pennylesse Pilgrimage* published in 1618.

But the gracious city, handsome though its main street might be, had a malodorous reputation – it stank of filth, human and animal, potting vegetables, rotting meat, and the dirt of its citizens. So much so that the Privy Council in 1619 remarked that it had now become 'filthie and uncleine, and the streetis, venallis, wyndis and cloisses thairoff overlayd and coverit with middingis'. People could not get a free passage to their lodgings because of the piles of rubbish then so universal that in the height of summer 'it corruptis the air, and gives greit occasioun of seikness'.

It was not doing Edinburgh much good from a public relations point of view as visitors protested at its state, calling the burgh 'a most filthie pudle of filth and uncleaness, the lyk quhairof is not to be seine in no pairt of the world'. The provost and magistrates were ordered to keep the closes, wynds and streets clean, with a constable to be appointed to supervise every close and see it was kept tidy.

From around this time, because of the habit of hurling slops from the uppermost windows to the street many storeys below, developed one of the street calls – 'Gardyloo' – from the French, 'watch out for the water'. A polite warning for the folk beneath that something mighty unpleasant was about to fall on them. The traditional reply was 'haud your hand' to give those below a chance to get out of the way. Less considerate residents dispensed with the warning, and a well-chosen target might be a revenge for some slight.

The lack of cleanliness spread to the citizens. Edward Burt, writing about 1740, recalls this experience: 'Being a stranger, I was invited to sup at a tavern. The cook was too filthy an object to be described; only, another English gentleman whispered me and said, he believed, if the fellow was thrown against the wall, he would stick to it. Twisting round and round his hand a greasy towel, he stood waiting to know what we would have for supper, and mentioned several things himself; among the rest a duke, a fool, and a meer-fool. This was nearly according to his pronunciation; but he meant, a duck, a fowl, and a moor-fowl or grouse.

> 'We supped very plentifully, and drank good French claret, and were very merry till the clock struck ten, the hour when every body is at liberty by beat of drum to throw filth out at the window. Then the company began to light pieces of paper, and throw them upon the table to smoke the room, and as I thought, to raise one bad smell with another.
>
> 'Being in my retreat to pass through a narrow wynde or alley, to go to my new lodgings, a guide was assigned to me, who went before me to prevent my disgrace, crying out all the way, 'Haud your haunde!' The throwing up of a sash or otherwise opening a window, made me tremble, while behind and before me, at some little distance, fell the terrible shower.
>
> 'Well, I escaped all danger, and arrived, not only safe and sound, but sweet and clean, at my new quarters; but when I was in bed, I was forced to hide my head between the sheets; for the smell of the filth thrown out by the neighbours at the back of the house, came pouring into the room to such a degree, I was almost poisoned with the stench.'

The year is 1774 and Captain Edward Topham is describing the style of building in the city as

> 'much like the French: the houses, however, in general are higher, as some rise to twelve, and one in particular to thirteen stories in height. But to the front of the street nine or ten stories is the common run; it is the back part of the edifice which, by being built on the slope of an hill, sinks to that amazing depth so as to form the above number . . . In general, however, the highest and lowest

tenements are possessd by artificers, while the gentry and better sort of people dwell in the fifth and sixth stories.

'In London you may know such an habitation would not be deemed the most eligible, and many a man in such a situation would not be sorry to descend a little lower. The style of building here has given rise to different ideas: Some years ago a Scotch gentleman, who went to London for the first time, took the uppermost

Tucked away in a back court off the Lawnmarket there's plenty of time to enjoy a quiet drink. The Old Town caters exceedingly well for those looking to eat or drink, with a wide range of restaurants, hostelries, and carry-out shops.

There's a Continental atmosphere abroad in Edinburgh with tables outside many public houses so visitors and locals can sit in the sun and watch the world go by. Liberal licensing laws mean too it's not hard to find a bar that's open at any time of the day.

141

story of a lodging-house, and was very much surprised to find what he thought the genteelest place of the whole at the lowest price. His friends who came to see him, in vain acquainted him with the mistake he had been guilty of; "He ken'd very weel," he said, "what gentility was, and after having lived all his life in a sixth story, he was not come to London to live upon the ground".'

Topham too had one complaint as a stranger – the dirt in the wynds:

'The magistrates, by imposing fines and other punishments, have long put a stop to the throwing any thing from the windows into the open street; but as these alleys are unlighted, narrow, and removed from public view, they still continue these practices with impunity. Many an elegant suit of clothes has been spoiled; many a powdered, well-dressed maccaroni sent home for the evening; and, to conclude this period in Doctor Johnson's own simple words, "many a full flowing periwig moistened into flaccidity".'

But life was improving in the eighteenth century, even though Robert Chambers says that at the beginning of George III's reign in 1760 Edinburgh was a 'picturesque, odorous, inconvenient, old fashioned town of about seventy thousand inhabitants'.
William Creech, the Luckenbooth publisher, who incidentally served on the jury at the Deacon Brodie trial and produced in record time an account of that experience, throws light on just what changes were taking place in the Old Town. He compares 1763 when Edinburgh had few hackney coaches, 'and perhaps the worst of the kind in Britain', with 1783 – 'The number of hackney coaches was more than tripled, and they were the handsomest carriages and had the best horses for the purpose of any, without exception, in Europe'. Civic pride from the man who was to become Lord Provost, or accurate reporting? Let's look at some of the other changes he recorded:

1763 – There was no such profession as perfumer: barbers and wigmakers were numerous, and were in the order of decent burgesses: Hairdressers were few, and hardly permitted to dress hair on Sundays; and many of them voluntarily decline it.
1783 – Perfumers had splendid shops in every principal street: Some of them advertised the keeping of bears to kill occasionally, for greasing ladies' and gentlemen's hair, as superior to any other animal fat. Hairdressers were more than tripled in number; and their busiest day was a Sunday. There was a professor who advertised a Hair-dressing Academy, and gave lectures on that noble and useful art.

Among items of people's habits, he notes:

In 1763 – People of fashion dined at two o'clock, or a little after it; – business was attended to in the afternoon. It was a common practice to lock the shops at one o'clock, and to open them after dinner at two.

In 1783 – People of fashion, and of the middle rank, dined at four or five o'clock: No business was done in the afternoon, dinner of itself having become a very serious business.

In 1763 – Wine was seldom seen, or, in a small quantity, at the tables of the middle rank of people.

In 1783 – Every tradesman in decent circumstances presents wine after dinner; and many in plenty and variety.

In 1763 – It was the fashion for gentlemen to attend the drawing rooms of the ladies in the afternoons, to drink tea, and to mix in the society and conversation of the women.

In 1783 – The drawing rooms were totally deserted; invitations to tea in the afternoon were given up; and the only opportunity the gentlemen had of being in ladies' company, was when they happened to mess together at dinner or supper; and, even then, an impatience was sometimes shown until the ladies retired. Card parties, after a long dinner and also after a late supper, were frequent.

In 1763 – A young man was termed a fine fellow, who, to a well-informed and an accomplished mind, added elegance of manners, and a conduct guided by principle; one who would not have injured the rights of the meanest individual; one who contracted no debts that he could not pay; and thought every breach of morality unbecoming the character of a gentleman; – who studied to be useful to society, so far as his opportunity or abilities enabled him.

In 1783 – The term fine fellow was applied to one who could drink three Bottles; who discharged all debts of honour, (or game debts and tavern bills), and evaded payment of every other; who swore immoderately, and before ladies, and talked of his word of honour; who ridiculed religion and morality as folly or hypocrisy, (but without argument); who was very jolly at the table of his friend, and would lose no opportunity of seducing his wife, or of debauching his daughter, if she was handsome; but, on the mention of such a thing being attempted to his own connections, would have cut the throat, or blown out the brains of his dearest companion, offering such an insult; – who was forward in all the fashionable follies of the time; who disregarded the interest of society, or the good of mankind, if they interfered with his own vicious selfish pursuits and pleasure.

Nor did Creech neglect the seamier side of life in his observations:

In 1763 – There were five or six brothels, or houses of bad fame, and a very few of the lowest and most ignorant order of females sculked about the streets at night. A person might have gone from the Castle to Holyroodhouse (the then length of the city), at any hour in the night without being accosted by a single street-walker. Street-robbery and pocket-picking were unknown.

In 1783 – The number of brothels had increased twenty-fold, and the women of the town more than a hundred-fold. Every quarter of the city and suburbs was infested with multitudes of females abandoned to vice, and a great many at a very early period of life, before passion could mislead, or reason teach them right from wrong. Street-robbing, pick-pockets, and thieves, had much increased.

Those 'ladies of pleasure' were so admired that in 1775 an 'impartial list' of their names, addresses and particular attractions was printed privately. Mrs Japp in Berringer's Close, for instance, 'enticed more young Nymphs to appear at the Shrine of Venus, than any priestess ever did in this City'. Miss Peggy McLean at Miss Adams's 'gentle temple' in Halkerston's Wynd was 'a very pretty girl, rather short, about 19 years of age, dark brown hair and very good teeth . . . and carries the luxury of love to the highest pitch,' writes our Casanova of the consumer guide.

The changing nature of the Old Town as leading citizens chose to cross the divide to live in the New Town was very marked. Creech again:

1783 – The Lord Justice Clerk Tinwald's House possessed by a French teacher – Lord President Craigie's house by a rouping wife or saleswoman of old furniture – and Lord Drummore's house left by a chairman for want of accommodation.

But there was still plenty of entertainment to be had among the closes. There were the various clubs which attracted their supporters – the Pious Club whose members met in a pie-shop; the Spendthrift Club where members pledged not to spend more than 4½d each night. The Lawnmarket Club was composed mostly of woollen traders who met about seven o'clock every morning and walked down to the post office to discover the news of the day. Then they adjourned to a public house for a sup of brandy. They were always the first in town with the news, and on Wednesdays when there was no post from London, they amused themselves by making it up and spreading it round town, their doubtful reports having the nickname of the 'Lawnmarket Gazette'. Many of the clubs were involved with drinking, accepted as a way of life from the highest to the lowest, and habits were regulated by what Allan Ramsay described as 'frae the gill-bells tae the drum'. The bells of St Giles struck half an hour before noon and these were the gill-bells 'from people's taking a whetting dram at that time, to ten o'clock at night, when the drum goes round to warn sober folks to call for the bill'. In the taverns and coffee houses much of the day's business was conducted and the tavern keepers were popular characters. Many of them were women or 'luckies' as they were called. Luckie Fykie could boast among her customers Lord Braxfield and other leading legal luminaries in her tiny place in the Potterrow, while down in the Canongate Lucky Wood was immortalised in verse by Allan Ramsay. Robert Fergusson also penned a tribute to his favourite landlady, Lucky Middlemass, whose tavern on the Cowgate is covered by a pier of the South Bridge.

> 'When big as burns the gutters rin,
> Gin ye hae catcht a droukit skin,
> To Luckie Middlemist's loup in,
> And sit fu' snug
> O'er oysters, and a dram o' gin,
> Or haddock lug.'

Then, as now, the taverns attracted their particular groups of customers. These days you can find the lawyers favouring one or two pubs in the High Street, while journalists prefer to keep to Fleshmarket Close, and the city councillors spread their custom. Over the clink of glasses and the sipping of coffee in the modern places of refreshment there is a growing awareness of the importance of the Old Town both for its position in the heart of the city as a place to live and its tremendous untapped tourist potential. There have been grievous mistakes with the wanton demolition of old buildings in the name of improvements, and a new sensitivity is abroad whenever development of any kind is mentioned. The Tailors' Hall site in the Cowgate is an instance where careful thought will have to be given to what happens next; just as the gap site in the Royal Mile between Niddry Street and Blackfriars Street remained derelict for many years before an acceptable development of hotel, flats and shops was found. What will happen to the Tron Kirk? And the huge site at Holyrood Brewery? More houses are being created and flats throughout the Old Town are steady sellers, although there are problems with parking and a certain amount of vandalism and noise in a city where pubs can be found open from seven in the morning until early the following day.

There is a vigilant Old Town Association, an amenity body for the Old Town Conservation Area. The Old Town Committee for Conservation and Renewal are based in Advocate's Close (page 43) with a full-time director and staff who are fighting to bring back the Old Town to a properly balanced life, ensuring that the

Another sketch by Walter Geikie of the Grassmarket with horse traders and pedlars at work. Geikie died in 1837 and is buried in Greyfriars Kirkyard.

old inhabitants are not driven out of what its director has called 'a very remarkable community, literally spanning dosser to aristocracy'. There is a delicate balance to be maintained between the developer, the existing inhabitant, the trendy incomer, and, of course, the tourist for whom multi-million-pound proposals are being canvassed. An active free community newspaper performs a very useful watchdog role, and vigorous housing groups are not slow to put forward their own views.

But areas like the Grassmarket, High Street, Canongate and the Cowgate must be sensibly redeveloped, and as part of an overall strategy, if the Old Town is not to lose its uniqueness. That is for the future; today there is a fascination in this part of the city which is there for anyone to go and discover.

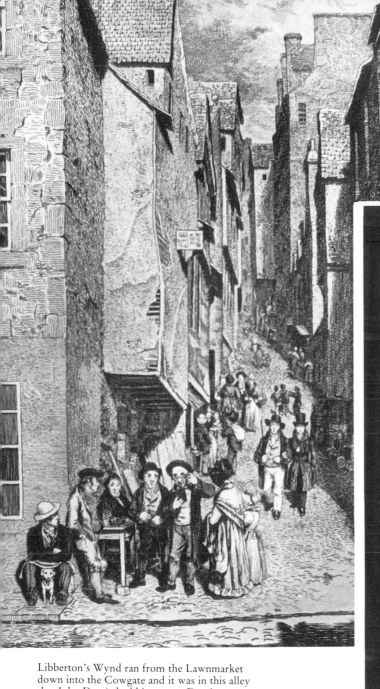

Libberton's Wynd ran from the Lawnmarket down into the Cowgate and it was in this alley that John Dowie had his tavern. Dowie ran a strict house and refused to serve another bottle after the bell on St Giles chimed midnight – ''tis past twelve and time to go home', he told his revellers.

Near the foot of the Canongate the message is clear. . .Edinburgh has a Jazz Festival along with all the other events of the year. A major redevelopment will take place soon between the Canongate and Holyrood Road with the clearing of the Holyrood Brewery site. Life goes on evolving in the Old Town. . .

CHAPTER *12*   R A I N Y D A Y S

*W*HILE THERE is a tremendous amount to see outdoors in the Old Town, there is always the problem of what to do when it rains. The most attractive closes in the sunshine take on a dreichness when the mist and rain whirl round the town, so here are some suggestions – in alphabetical order – for where you can pass an hour or two and at the same time add something to your knowledge of life in the Old Town.

Bank of Scotland Head Office, The Mound – Museum showing various aspects of the bank, founded in 1695, one year after the Bank of England.
Open July 1 to September 30 during banking hours. Other times by arrangement. Free.
Contact the bank's head office at the Mound, 'phone 243-5830.

Brass Rubbing Centre, Trinity Apse, Chalmers Close, High Street – A collection of replicas moulded from Pictish stones, medieval church brasses, and rare Scottish brasses can be copied. There is an ample supply of materials needed to take the rubbings, and the cost is dependent on the brass selected. Shop.
Open Monday to Saturday 10am to 5pm.
June to September 10am to 6pm.
Festival Sundays 2-5pm. Admission free.

Canongate Kirk – Open daily from July to the end of the Festival for visitors. A lovely and unusual building with many interesting paintings, pictures and banners. Kirkyard contains many well-known persons including George Drummond, Burns' 'Clarinda', Adam Smith and poet Robert Fergusson.
Sunday services – 10am family worship; 11am morning worship.
The minister also leads the dawn service at the top of Arthur's Seat on May 1.

Canongate Tolbooth – Featuring The People's Story. A dramatic exhibition opened in the summer of 1989 to show visitors what life in the city was like in the past through a series of reconstructions – a prison cell, a cooper's workshop, draper's shop, a steamie (wash-house), tearoom and other vignettes. An outstanding collection of trade union banners. Shop.
Open Monday to Saturday 10am to 5pm.
June to September 10am to 6pm.
Festival Sundays 2-5pm. Free.

The Castle – Edinburgh's biggest tourist attraction with the lovely St Margaret's Chapel and the Scottish National War Memorial among the top interests for the visitor.
Guides available. Shop.
Open Monday to Saturday 9.30am to 5.05pm, last admission.
Sunday 11am to 5.05pm, last admission.

Admission – Adult £2.30; child, OAP £1.10; family ticket £5.

City Art Centre, Market Street – A converted fruit warehouse was the site of record-breaking exhibitions like the Gold of the Pharaohs and the Chinese Warriors. There are various exhibitions all the year round in this award-winning building which provides a permanent home for the city's collection of Scottish paintings, drawings, prints and sculptures. Shop and cafe.
Open Monday to Saturday 10am to 5pm.
June to September 10am to 6pm. Free, except for some special exhibitions and displays.

Edinburgh Room, Central Library, George IV Bridge – For the student of Old Edinburgh, amateur or professional, there is no better starting point. An exhaustive index points the way to thousands of documents, books, newspapers, cuttings and maps. An Aladdin's cave of information manned by a helpful and knowledgeable staff. Library shop.
Open Monday to Friday 9am to 9pm.
Saturday 9am to 1pm. Free.

Fruitmarket Galley, Market Street – Various exhibitions of contemporary art. Cafe.
Open Tuesday to Saturday 10am to 5.30pm.
Sunday 1.30pm to 5.30pm.

Gladstone's Land, Lawnmarket – How a prosperous merchant lived in the seventeenth century in the property now owned by the National Trust for Scotland.
Open April 1 to October 31.
Monday to Saturday 10am to 5pm.
Sunday 2-5pm.
Admission – Adults £1.60; children and OAP 80p. Free guided walk from Gladstone's Lane to the Georgian House in Charlotte Square in season.

Greyfriars Kirk (strictly Greyfriars Tolbooth and Highland), top of Candlemaker Row – Copy of the National Covenant and other Covenanting relics inside the building which was undergoing major restoration in 1989. The kirkyard has some of the finest examples of monumental sculpture in Scotland, and also contains the resting place of many famous figures in the nation's history.
Gaelic service every Sunday at 3pm, in addition to 11am worship.
Church open April to September, kirkyard open daily 8am to 4pm.

Holyrood Palace – The Queen's official residence in the city, and full of memories of the ill-fated Mary Queen of Scots.
Open Monday to Saturday 9.30am to 5.15pm.
Sundays 10.30am to 4.30pm. Closed during Royal visit in July.
Guided tour of state and historic apartments. Abbey ruins.
Admission – Adults £1.80; child, OAP and students £1.

Huntly House, Canongate – Collection of Edinburgh's life in the city's principal museum of local history. Some superb shop signs, glass, pottery, silverware and mementoes of Earl Haig.
Open Monday to Saturday 10am to 5pm.

June to September 10am to 6pm.
Festival Sundays 2-5pm. Free.

John Knox's House, High Street – Traditionally connected with the minister of St Giles and great Reformer. Also incorporates the Old Town inquiry centre. Video showings.
Open Monday to Saturday 10am to 5pm, last admission to the house at 4.30pm.
Admission – Adults £1; children 70p.

Lady Stair's House, Lawnmarket – Portraits, relics and manuscripts of the literary
triumvirate of Robert Burns, Sir Walter Scott and Robert Louis Stevenson.
Open Monday to Saturday 10am to 5pm.
June to September 10am to 6pm.
Festival Sundays 2-5pm. Free.

Magdalen Chapel, Cowgate – It may be possible to arrange a visit. Contact Scottish
Reformation Society, George IV Bridge.

Museum of Childhood, High Street – A fascinating collection of the paraphernalia of
growing up. A treasure trove of children's toys and costumes, a place for the young
in heart of all ages. Children are definitely allowed to take their mums and dads to
this least 'museumy' of all the attractions in the Old Town. And that's a fitting tribute
to its instigator Patrick Murray, a former town councillor and the museum's first
curator. Museum shop.
Open Monday to Saturday 10am to 6pm.
October to May 10am to 5pm.
Sundays 2-5pm. Free.

National Library of Scotland, George IV Bridge – The basis of the library was the
foundation in 1689 of the Faculty of Advocates' Library. The National Library
was formed in 1925 and there are some five million books, plus a vast reservoir of
documents including Mary Queen of Scots' last letter. The reading rooms are open
for casual browsing and deeper research. There is usually an exhibition on display.
Sales counter.
Open Monday to Friday 9.30am to 8.30pm.
Saturday 9.30am to 1pm.

Netherbow Arts Centre, High Street – Frequent exhibitions, plus wide range of work
in theatre area.
Galleries open Monday to Saturday 10am to 4.30pm. Cafe. Free.

Outlook Tower and Camera Obscura, Castle Hill – Fascinating views of Edinburgh
from the camera which revolves to bring periscope living images of the city below.
Also superb views from the rooftop terrace. Holography display and exhibition of
pinhole photography. Shop.
Open Monday to Friday 9.30am to 6pm.
Saturday and Sunday 10am to 6pm.
Admission – Adults £1.90; children and OAP 90p.

Rainy Days

Parliament House – The seat of the Scottish High Court and Court of Session. Open Tuesday to Friday 9.30am to 4.30pm. Free.

Patrick Geddes Centre for Planning Studies, Outlook Tower – It is planned to create an archive of documents pertaining to the great town planner and architect. Material from the library at the former Association for Planning and Reconstruction and more recent plans relative to Scotland.
Visitors by appointment during office hours. Contact 20 Chambers Street, or 'phone 667-1011, ext 4555/4551.

Portfolio Gallery and Photographic Workshop, 43 Candlemaker Row – A place to encourage the development of new Scottish photography. Exhibitions and workshops.
Workshop and bookshop open Monday to Saturday 11am to 5.30pm.
Gallery open Tuesday to Saturday 11am to 5.0pm.
During the Festival open seven days. Free.

Richard Demarco Gallery, Blackfriars Street – Home of Edinburgh's probably best-known entrepreneur in the Edinburgh arts field – and far beyond. Wide range of exhibitions in the old church building which occupies the site of the medieval Dominican monastery.
Open Monday to Saturday 10.30am to 6pm. Free.

Royal Museum of Scotland, Chambers Street – One of the finest examples of Victorian architecture in Edinburgh. Specialised exhibitions in addition to a tremendous variety of permanent displays. Shop and cafe.
Open Monday to Saturday 10am to 5pm.
Sunday 2-5pm. Free.

St Cecilia's Hall, Cowgate – Russell Collection of harpsichords and clavichords.
Open Wednesday and Saturday 2-5pm.
During Festival Monday to Saturday 10am to 12.30pm. Admission 25p.

St Giles, High Kirk of Edinburgh, High Street – Worshippers and visitors equally welcome. Public worship Monday to Saturday at noon; Sunday 8am, 10am, 11.30am, 6pm and 8pm.
Open Monday to Saturday 9am to 5pm (7pm in summer). Free. Shop and cafe.
Thistle Chapel, Admission adult 30p, child, student and OAP 5p.

The Scotch Whisky Heritage Centre, Castle Hill – 'A voyage through time that brings the history, mystery and the magic of Scotch whisky to life.' A travel through time on an electric car unveils the traditions and myths about our national drink – commentary in English, Dutch, French, German, Italian, Japanese and Spanish.
Open seven days a week, 10am to 5pm, 9am to 6.30pm June to September.
Admission adult £2.50, student £2, OAP £1.50, children 5-16 £1.25, family ticket £6.50.

Scottish Craft Centre, Acheson House, 140 Canongate – A showplace for the Scottish heritage in fine workmanship and design of a wide range of crafts. Periodic exhibitions.
Open Monday to Saturday 10am to 5.30pm. Free.

Scottish Poetry Library, Tweeddale Court, High Street – Centre for promoting poetry in Scotland and for research and information. Collections in Gaelic, Scots and English of books, tapes and magazines.
Open Monday to Saturday noon to 6pm.
Thursday 2-8pm. Free.

Stills Photography Gallery and Workshop, 105 High Street – Scotland's leading specialist photography gallery founded in 1977 by the Scottish Photography Group.
Bookshop
Open Tuesday to Saturday 11am to 5.30pm. Free.

Talbot Rice Art Centre, Old College – The University art collection. Permanent collection on display. Exhibitions as advertised.
Open Tuesday to Saturday 10am to 5pm. Free.

369 Gallery, 233 Cowgate – Scottish contemporary paintings.
Open Monday to Saturday 10am to 5.30pm. Free.

Tron Kirk, High Street – Open during the summer with special Old Town exhibitions. The exposed Marlin's Wynd is a fascinating scrap of sixteenth-century Edinburgh which has been preserved.

There are many other entertainments in the Old Town. You can find an evening of medieval banqueting, or invest a pound or two in a night exploring the haunted closes with strange goings-on appearing in darkened corners. There are walking tours, or

Rainy Days   you can find two strong men to carry you around in a sedan chair. In the old days a bunch of youngsters called the 'cadies' were hired to guide visitors round the town and to run messages, and their modern-day equivalents are ready to provide such services for the tourist.

There are good restaurants and water holes, cafes and a wide range of carry-out foods in the New Town.

It's worth scanning the advertisements in the local papers to check on exhibitions and other events. The Festival Fringe office in the High Street issues a free brochure of the jamboree of shows during the Festival, and also organises a Fringe Sunday in Holyrood Park where an afternoon of non-stop entertainment by enthusiastic performers defies any weather.

The list above gives a few ideas on how to spend a rainy day; please check out the times and admission prices in case they have altered.

FURTHER READING

William Anderson: *The Poor of Edinburgh and their Homes*
Hugo Arnot: *The History of Edinburgh*
G.P. Black: *Arthur's Seat*
Books of the Old Edinburgh Club
Robert Chambers: *Traditions of Edinburgh*
Robert Chambers: *Fires in Edinburgh*
Lord Cockburn: *Memorials of His Own Time*
William Creech: *Fugitive Pieces*
Lord Cullen: *The Walls of Edinburgh*
James Grant: *Old and New Edinburgh*
HMSO: *An Inventory of the Ancient and Historical Monuments of the City of Edinburgh*
David Keir: *The Younger Centuries*
Forbes Macgregor: *The Story of Greyfriars Bobby*
John Mackay: *History of the Burgh of Canongate*
Charles McKean: *Edinburgh: An Illustrated Architectural Guide*
Ed. Colin McWilliam: *The Buildings of Scotland: Edinburgh*
David Robertson and Marguerite Wood: *Castle and Town*
Ed. William Roughead: *Burke and Hare (Notable British Trials)*
Sir Walter Scott: *Tales of a Grandfather*
Robert T. Skinner: *The Royal Mile*
Robert Louis Stevenson: *Edinburgh Picturesque Notes*
Marie W. Stuart: *Old Edinburgh Taverns*
Sir Daniel Wilson: *Memorial of Edinburgh in the Olden Time*

Index